PEACEMAKING AND THE IMMORAL WAR:

PEACEMAKING AND THE IMMORAL WAR:

ARABS AND JEWS IN THE MIDDLE EAST

Elias H. Tuma

Harper & Row, Publishers
New York, Evanston,
San Francisco,
London

LIBRARY OF CONGRESS CATALOG CARD NUMBER: 71–189634

STANDARD BOOK NUMBER: 06–1360872

*To the Arabs and Israelis
who have suffered through the folly
and misjudgement of others*

CONTENTS

PREFACE

It has been almost twenty years since the thoughts contained in this book were conceived. At that time I began addressing questions to both Arabs and Israelis regarding this seemingly unending conflict. Today I am no more convinced of the validity of their answers than I was then. Indeed, their arguments have become self-perpetuating, and hence the conflict becomes equally perennial. This deadlock must be broken before progress toward an acceptable solution can be made. I have lived through the conflict as a man in the middle, having addressed my questions to both parties and having tried to defend each side as the occasion permitted. I am convinced that it is high time for both the Arabs and the Israelis to face reality, to recognize their responsibilities, and to agree to make the necessary sacrifices for the peace and harmony they have been searching for. The thoughts expressed in this book, hopefully, will be useful to them in these efforts.

I am indebted to many Arab and Israeli friends who have debated the issues with me and kept up the challenge which has led me to write. I am also indebted to the American

Friends Peace Conference which discussed an earlier version of the manuscript and added encouragement to my efforts. Calvin Schwabe and Farhat Ziadeh made helpful comments for which I am grateful. I am also grateful to Mrs. Marguerite Crown for typing the manuscript. Last, but not least, I am grateful to Hugh Van Dusen and his staff and to Lynne McNabb, all of them from Harper & Row, for the excellent editorial and production job they have done on this book.

The thoughts, the hopes, and even the disappointments expressed in this book are mine alone as are the responsibilities that go with them.

Davis, California   E.H.T.
December 20, 1971

PEACEMAKING AND THE IMMORAL WAR:

Chapter 1 | Introduction

It is almost a century since the Jews conceived the idea of a national home, and soon thereafter Palestine became the target area of that idea. It was about that time that the Arabs became conscious of the impending danger to their national integrity, even though that integrity had not been rescued yet from the chains of foreign domination. It has been about half a century since the impending danger became a reality and a Jewish national home in Palestine became a possibility. The Balfour Declaration of 1917 was actually a declaration of the immoral war between Semites. It is doubtful whether the founders of Israel wanted a war, much less an immoral war. It is equally doubtful that the Arabs, or their spokesmen at that time, believed that they would be engaged in such an extensive, incurable, and immoral war. But it is not mere fate that has brought about the war: The Arabs and the Jews are responsible. Outside forces share that responsibility but only in a secondary degree. The seeds of the immorality of the war were sown early, and the conflict that has grown between two semitic peoples has generated enough antagonism and hatred so as to render peacemaking at the present time a

1

futile effort. Peace in the Middle East, who wants it? I venture to say that Gunnar Jarring wants it, but few other world leaders and policy-makers want it. Most of the common people are misinformed or have little to say about the war. So far, at least, they have followed their leaders or have chosen new leaders who follow policies similar to those of their predecessors.

Some may not agree with the description of the war as immoral, but they can hardly disagree with the facts of the war. The Arab-Israeli war is immoral because it is based on ignorance of the issues; it is a war that no one can actually win, a war that penalizes innocent people who had and have little to do with the conflict and that has become an outlet for antagonistic interactions between external powers with little or no direct concern for either Arabs or Jews. Peacemaking seems futile because of the widespread untruthfulness and hypocrisy on all sides of the conflict. The policy-makers, if they say anything, do not say what they mean and rarely mean what they say; they hide discrepancies under the vague concept of diplomacy. Yet, the war goes on, hatred mounts; a new round of fighting looms on the horizon, and meaningless talks about peace continue. We can only wonder whether either party really wants peace, and if they do, at what cost. It is not true that there is no solution, but neither side can actually win. Nor is it true that both sides are trying for a solution, although they talk about it constantly. It is apparent that each side has become so deeply immersed in this immoral war that it has almost become a way of life.

The reader will wonder by what right this indictment is made and what concern the author has in this dilemma. My concern stems from the fact that I am an Arab, was born in Palestine, and from 1948 to 1969 held an Israeli citizenship. I grew up with the Arab-Jewish-British conflict and certain incidents hang on vividly in my memory. At the age of eight

I saw Arab rebels (Thuwārs) lead a man to the outskirts of the village. They had gone hardly a mile (I could see them from the roof of the house) before they shot him dead, allegedly for spying and for collaborating with the British. Shortly thereafter, another man was found about two miles from the village. He had been dead for three days. I still remember the horrible sight of his body with the head smashed. His guilt was that his brother had been a policeman for 15 years; therefore, or so the argument went, he was a collaborator and a traitor. It soon became known that both men were killed for personal grudges. Neither was brought to trial, and no evidence was uncovered, but both were condemned in the name of Palestine and national independence. In 1947 and 1948 I saw mercenary Arabs take control of whole villages in the Galilee in Palestine, demoralize the people by taxing them heavily, and then lose the villages and even their own weapons to the enemies without fighting. Local people could do nothing, and the Palestinian leaders were too involved in feuds to care.

When I was 19, Jewish terrorists ambushed a bus on which I was riding at 5:30 a.m. on my way to work in Haifa. Six commuters were injured, including the driver. Only luck saved us. The person sitting next to me suffered the most severe injury and was hospitalized for weeks. In that same period I watched Arab leaders evacuate homes and villages, some long before Jewish attacks began. I also heard Jewish leaders ask them to stay and live peacefully with the Jews. I was in Haifa when the mayor pleaded with the Arab inhabitants to stay, but they panicked and left. I saw them leave the city in little boats, tightly packed like sardines, en route to Acre and from there to Lebannon. But I have also seen Israeli armed forces level villages, make mass arrests, scare away large groups of people, and exile Arabs summarily for months without trial.

I grew up among Arabs, but I also worked with Jews, lived among them, spoke their language, and made many friends who have left great impressions on me. I have seen German Jews who only wanted a home. They were happy to have me as a friend—an Arab friend. I have also seen Jews who had just arrived from Iraq and Morocco. They were unhappy and even bitter at the treatment they had received before leaving for Israel. Neither Arabs nor Jews can be proud of the way they treated each other.

At present I have family, relatives, and friends in Israel and in the Arab countries. Some have remained in Israel because they did not want to become refugees. I do not think they have regretted that decision, although the emotional cost has been high. Others left and were homeless for a while, but they have adjusted and succeeded in rehabilitating themselves. I do not think they have regretted their decision to depart, but they are unhappy because they lost homes and property.

My concern, however, is only partly subjective. I am interested in a settlement for the Arab-Israeli conflict as an international and human problem. As a man in the middle, I have been in contact with both sides. I have had chances to hear them both and have come face-to-face with the problem more than once. I have observed the loss of human capital by Jews and Arabs alike. I have seen emotions rise, reason subside, and all hopes of understanding vanish. Yet, all need not be lost. I think there is hope, and it is time that we take a fresh look at the situation in search of a meaningful and acceptable solution. I am convinced that neither side is all wrong or all right. I am also convinced that no solution can be fully acceptable to both sides. I am sure that no peace can be achieved without some compromise by both parties to the conflict. But I am also convinced that there is a solution, a settlement, and a chance for the suffering of the whole region to come to an end. This is an attempt to participate in the search.

Much has been written about the Arab-Israeli conflict, and little has been left unsaid. Unfortunately, the theme has always been to dramatize the conflict as very complex and difficult to resolve. Most writers usually attempt such sophistication in expressing the complexity that their analyses complicate rather than simplify the issues. The solution has little to do with whether the analysis is complex or not. When Mendes-France decided to end the war in Indo-China, it was ended. When de Gaulle decided to end the war in Algeria, it also was ended. And when Soviet Russia and the United States insisted on resolving the 1956 Suez crisis, it was quickly resolved. Where there is a will there is a way, regardless of the complexity of the problem or the sophistication of the analysis. I shall try in this context to simplify, rather than to complicate; I shall focus on substance, rather than on procedure, and I shall approach both Arabs and Israelis as one of them. With simplicity and brevity, we come closer to a solution.

In the next chapter I shall explain and illustrate the immorality of the war by evaluating the behavior of the parties to the conflict and that of their outside supporters. I shall then demonstrate the futility of the peacemaking efforts which have been based on half-truths and expediency and which therefore could not have led to peace. I will then propose a plan for peace, to be followed with some reflections on the future of these divided Semitic peoples of the Middle East.

Chapter 2 | The Immoral War

I

The war in the Middle East is immoral because of the distorted grounds on which it is based, the inhumane principles it fosters, and the impossibility of one side winning. Were the facts known, it would be considered immoral by both Arabs and Jews. The Jewish, Israeli, and Zionist justifications for the war distort the real issues because a national home for the Jews could have been created by alternative approaches, without war. The Arab reasons for fostering the war are trivial and cannot justify a war which they neither can afford nor win. The reasons given by other nations for allying themselves with Arabs or Israelis are fictitious; the true reasons are not publicized and are little different from those of classical imperialism. The immorality of the war is so commonplace that innocent supporters of moral and humane causes have become blinded to the facts. They support Arabs or Jews because they want to aid other human beings who need help. Yet those same Arabs and Jews readily go to war against each other and undermine all efforts to reach a peaceful solution. The war is also immoral from a functional materialistic standpoint: Resources that are badly needed in and outside the Middle East are being used in a wasteful war, at the expense of basic needs and sometimes of even mere subsistence.

These criteria of immorality are somewhat arbitrary and may be challenged. I have, therefore, invoked a relative approach according to which I will regard as immoral that which the members of societies under consideration regard as immoral in their public codes of ethics. Immorality here means that were the facts about policy and war activity known, these policies would be in conflict with the moral standards of the societies in question. More specifically, both Arabs and Jews claim that they are opposed to aggression; that they are defending their national homes; that they are searching for peace, justice, and humane solutions; that they had no alternatives to war, and that they would be willing to make sacrifices to promote peace and harmony. If the facts of the situation appeared to be in conflict with these standards, the war and the policies dictating it would be judged immoral. I suggest that the war between the Arabs and the Israelis is immoral from the point of view of both national groups.

Many people will disagree with this assessment. Some will appeal to dignity and honor which, according to them, can only be protected or restored by a war, regardless of the cost. Others will claim that they have been deprived of their lawful rights and that only war can retrieve lost heritage and redress grievances. Still others will claim that their action is defensive and that a small war seems necessary to prevent a bigger war. The most effective but untrue call to war is the one which contends that the mere existence of one of the parties is threatened and that war is the only way to prevent its annihilation. I suggest that these claims are exaggerated;

that they are expedient ways of recruiting support, and that the war is neither necessary nor the most efficient way of realizing basic objectives. Therefore, it is an immoral war.

A few fundamental questions should be raised at this juncture. Is there such a thing as a moral war? Is it not true that war is a means to an end and, therefore, cannot be classified as moral or immoral except in the context of the end itself? Is there a general or universal standard of morality that we can use in this evaluation? These controversial questions have plagued man throughout most of his history. Different schools of thought have suggested answers that are partially acceptable, but to my knowledge, none has solved the problem on a general basis. Probably the simplest answer to these questions is embodied in the maxim "might makes right." Hence, so the argument goes, if one succeeds and is powerful, he prescribes the laws of morality for his contemporaries. This philosophy, implicitly or explicitly, has prevailed for centuries. No doubt it has also characterized the conflict in the Middle East, but no one will admit it. More "respectable" justifications of war include the defense of freedom, the preservation of human values, defense of self and homeland, and so on. Rousseau thus would justify a revolution to preserve democracy and the general will. Marx would regard a class war as a natural course to secure freedom from exploitation. Bertrand Russell felt justified in opposing World War I as immoral but was less inclined to oppose World War II because he was opposed to Hitler and to fascism. The United Nations justifies war in defense of sovereignty and national boundaries, but what happens once national boundaries have been changed by occupation is not clear. (The God of the Hebrews would smite their enemies, and Islam would be spread by the sword in a holy war, or Jihād.)

These justifications have one feature in common: They all regard war as just if it is to preserve national and human values. If freedom is one of these values, it should be defended—even by invading the territory of the potential enemy, as implied by a preventive or deterrent war. These approaches implicitly suggest that war can succeed in realizing these objectives and that no better or more efficient means is available. If so, we may arrive at a definition of what may be considered a morally justifiable war. War can be morally justifiable if it preserves and defends, if it succeeds as a preservative or defensive measure, and if it is the most efficient or least costly way of preserving or defending the given values or objectives.

By these criteria the war in the Middle East fails to pass the test of morality as the following analysis will show. (The degree to which the war fails to meet the test may have changed several times since the beginning of the conflict because the objectives of the war have undergone transformation in the meantime.)

Strictly speaking, the war between the Arabs and Israelis began in 1948 when the State of Israel was established. The conflict, however, goes back to the last quarter of the nineteenth century when Herzl conceived the idea of a national home for the Jews and Palestine became the target area for that home. For more than half a century the Arabs and the Jews were governed by outsiders, first by Turkey and then by Britain as the mandate government. Both rebelled against Britain, but they were not very friendly to each other. The seeds of conflict and the grounds for this immoral war were sown before 1948. The claims, counterclaims, and distortions which have poisoned all efforts to create harmony were initiated in that period. Therefore, to put the present war into proper perspective, I shall review the early history of the conflict and point out the half-truths and untruths on which warmongering has been nourished and by which it is still reinforced.

Let me first remove some common misconceptions. The conflict between Arabs and Jews, before and after the establishment of the State of Israel, is not a racial war. Both are Semitic peoples and anti-Semitism cannot be implied meaningfully in the conflict. The concept of anti-Semitism has been used as a catchword for the condemnation of acts against Jews, Israelis, and Zionists. It has sometimes been used to condemn acts that are pro-Arab, even though they may not be against Jews. This confusion is one of the reasons for antagonism between the Arab countries and the Western world. The confusion surrounding the concept of anti-Semitism is partly a play on words for political and propoganda reasons and an attempt to gain sympathy for the State of Israel. However, it is sometimes a result of latent fears among Jews. Seymour Martin Lipset, for instance, admits the difficulty of distinguishing between anti-Semitic and non-anti-Semitic actions; yet he goes on to brand all shades of anti-Jewish, anti-Zionist, anti-Israeli, or pro-Arab as possibly or potentially anti-Semitic.[1]

The conflict is not religious. Neither are all Arabs of one religion, nor are all Jews religious. Neither group can seriously claim that the conflict is based on religion, although this is often done for expediency. The conflict is not based on differences in political beliefs or systems, even though such differences may seem apparent and are frequently dramatized by external powers for their own purposes. The Arab countries and Israel both have welfare programs which render their economic systems mixed between capitalism and socialism; these systems are also in the process of continuous change.

[1]For etymology of the concept see William Ward, "Semantics of Anti-Semitism," *Middle East Newsletter*, vol. 3, no. 4 (May–June 1969); on the latent fears see Seymour Martin Lipset, "The Socialism of Fools," *New York Times Magazine*, Jan. 3, 1971.

The conflict is basically territorial, although other sources of conflict by now have developed into independent causes of antagonism, distrust, and possibly deep hatred between Arabs and Jews. The conflict has been aggravated by the claims and counterclaims of both groups and by the means used to realize their conflicting objectives. I should add that these claims, regardless of their truthfulness or justness, have been fanned by external forces to the extent that retreat by either party seems unthinkable.

II

The Jewish claims to Palestine provided the basis for the conflict. Before the establishment of Israel, the Jewish aim was to secure territory, and after it had been secured, to defend it and, according to some observers, to expand it. Why have the Jews made a claim for Palestine in particular or for any territory at all? Would not some other alternative solution have been possible? The Zionist idea, as conceived by Herzl, was to create a Jewish national home that would give the Jews security and protection from the persecution they had suffered so often. A place of refuge was the main objective. The choice of Palestine was an afterthought. In fact, Herzl was not sold on the idea because other territories would have served the same objective and probably at a lower cost than has been the case with Palestine. Why, then, have other Zionist leaders and Gentile supporters pursued the choice of Palestine in the face of local opposition?

The claim for Palestine has been backed by various arguments. First, Palestine was historically Jewish, and the Jews therefore would be repatriated to a national home. What an absurd idea! It supposes that the Arabs, who had been in Palestine for many centuries, surrender their land to the

Jews, who once were in Palestine, even though the Arabs had little to do with the discontinuity in Jewish history. If this claim has any logic to it, then the Arabs should take Spain, the whole Mediterranean, and parts of Iran and Pakistan; Turkey should restore its lost empire; the American Indians should recover the Americas, and the blacks of America should go back and claim Africa. The theory of historical rights, vague as it is, could lead to nothing other than chaos and infinite absurdity. The Jews cannot claim Palestine on historical grounds without giving credence to the claims of the Palestinian Arabs to the Palestine they lost only two decades ago. The two claims for Palestine cannot be reconciled, and the war can have no end in view. Nor can the war be justified as moral by such contradictory claims.

A more widespread but equally ridiculous claim is religious. Jews everywhere are told, and Gentiles seem to agree, that Palestine is Jewish, and therefore the Jews should have the right to return to their holy land. The land may be holy, and the Jews may regard it sacred, but their claim is neither sacred nor unique. In fact, their claim has no more validity than claims of other religions for the same territory. Palestine is equally holy for Moslems and Christians. Moslems, in fact, have established major religious sites in various parts of the country, as have Christians. If any of these religious affiliates has a claim, all of them do. And if all have equally valid claims, the land should be held by all or should be free and open to all. Neither approach is consistent with the Jewish religious claim to Palestine. Furthermore, how can the religious claim be justified when many early Zionist leaders were atheists and more than 50 percent of the Israelis are not religious? Whether in Palestine or elsewhere, all that counts is to have a national home! Were Palestine so attractive to the Jews on religious grounds, why have the vast majority of Jews in the world, including religious groups, cared little about emigrating to the promised land? Indeed, Herzl, among others, welcomed the British offer of territory in Uganda as a place for a Jewish state.

Why, then, was Palestine chosen as the target area for the creation of a Jewish national home? Simply put, it was chosen because it seemed expedient; it looked like easy prey, and it relieved the western powers of any obligation to open their own gates for Jewish immigration. Furthermore, they found in the creation of a Jewish state in Palestine a convenient way of guarding and promoting their own interests in Asia and the Middle East. These explanations applied throughout the pre-1948 period, and since then there has been no need for explanation. The policy has changed from securing the territory to defending it.

The choice of Palestine seemed expedient because of its international appeal. It appealed to Jews all over the world. Whether by invoking history or religion, promoters of the idea correctly forecast how appealing it would be, at least to recruit material support if not immigrants. Furthermore, Palestine seemed appealing because it was under the rule of a declining power and because the Palestinian Arabs were not as yet highly nationalistic or equipped to defend the security of their land. In other words, it was expedient to take advantage of the weakness of the defenders of Palestine and to establish a Jewish national home against their wishes. It is true that until the end of World War I the Jewish settlement in Palestine was sparse, not greatly political, and did not seem to pose a threat to the native Arab population. The expediency of the choice, as well as the reality of the threat, was dramatically announced in the Balfour Declaration of 1917, which promised to realize a Jewish national home in Palestine. Palestine was attractive not only because of historical and religious backgrounds, but also because of the apparent low cost at which it could be secured with the help of the ruling power. In fact, the western powers were happy to be generous by awarding territory that did not belong to them. Zionist claims were thus enhanced by the ready support of the western powers. The Jewish leaders did not need to worry about the people of Palestine because someone else would worry for them. The immorality of these dealings and the meaningless appeals to history and religion did not seem to bother anyone's conscience. Even if blood were to be shed, the end seemed to justify the means. At least one part of Palestine was finally secured, and the State of Israel was created.

Once the state had been established, the claims to its secure existence became political, not merely historical or religious. The people of the state had the right to defend the integrity of their political entity and to guard their national boundaries, regardless of the truth or falseness of the grounds on which the state was founded.

Since then, the policies of the Israeli leaders have changed only in form, not in substance or truthfulness. Israel has been involved in war since its creation. We now are told that Israel is only defending its integrity and that the war is the responsibility of the Arab aggressors. We are told that Israel is not expansionist in character and is no longer seeking territory. We are told also that Israel has the right to safeguard the security of the desert they have converted into blooming gardens and the mountains they have turned into highly productive agricultural land. This constructivist achievement seems to have an appeal especially in America where self-help in opening the frontierland, at the expense of the Indians, was highly acclaimed. Yet these claims are half true or not true at all. Finally, the state is defended on the grounds that the Jews now have a national home, dignity, and independence, values which cannot be compromised. Nothing is said about the effects of these new achievements on others.

The Arabs may have fired the first shot in the war with Israel, but one can hardly ignore Israel's long history of encroachment on the territory and the impending danger of its expansion. One can hardly agree that the war has been defensive when one recalls that the invasion of Suez in 1956 was not to defend the state boundaries or to guarantee the security and dignity of the Jewish people. Nor indeed was the war of 1967, for which the Israeli army prepared for ten years, a defense of national boundaries. It has been argued that the war was imminent and that, therefore, Israel had no alternative but to take the initiative in order to turn the odds in its favor.

These arguments might be accepted as true had Israel not taken advantage of these wars to expand its territory by occupation. Expansionism has been recurrent in the policy declarations of various Jewish or Zionist groups, and actual expansionism has been an integral feature of the history of the State of Israel since its creation. In 1948, Israel occupied territories beyond the boundaries specified by the United Nations for the State of Israel. After the war, Israel stayed. In 1956, Israel was anxious to stay on the bank of the Suez Canal; the United States, Soviet Russia, and the United Nations made this impossible by pressuring Britain and France to withdraw; Israel could not stay alone. The gains made in 1967 have remained in the hands of Israel. No commitment to withdrawal has been made. In fact, statements are made to the contrary, a return to the pre-1967 boundaries is declared inconceivable for security reasons. Still we hear of the nonexpansionist tendencies or intentions and of the absence of any warmongering on the part of Israel. War continues and additional arguments are fabricated to sustain it. How much more immoral can the war be: It has been carried to the neighboring territory; new lands are occupied and retained; more people are dislocated and turned into homeless refugees; capital is used in nonproductive investments in a region in which poverty is still the rule rather than the exception. Nonetheless, we are supposed to regard the war activity as merely defensive. The West is sold on the idea. No doubt the West has reasons of its own.

It is not true that the Jews in Palestine developed the land where the Arabs did nothing. It is true that Jewish settlement and agriculture were great achievements, but it is also true that the Arabs developed highly advanced farms and orchards. In fact, relative to the capital available to each, the Arabs probably achieved more than the Jews. With much less capital and skill, the Arabs developed high competitive citrus and olive production. Tobacco and grains also were fully developed. It is not totally correct to say that development of the land was one-sided. And even if it were correct, does development entitle the developer to political rights at the expense of the nondeveloper?

The most immoral explanation in defense of the state policy lies in the claim that the Jews needed a refuge, a national home, and security from persecution, all of which are now embodied in the state of Israel and must be defended. That the Jews needed these achievements is incontestable, but is it moral to settle one people by dislocating another? Is it humane to offer refuge to one people and make refugees of another? Is it defensible to create a national home for one people by depriving another of their home and land? Israel cannot absolve itself of these contradictions by shifting the responsibility to others. Israel has relocated one million people by dislocating as many, while blaming the Arabs for not cooperating and for not conforming with the objectives of the Israeli state. The fact of the matter is that the only justification of the Israeli policy is might; military occupation seems to overcome all other arguments and to invite support by appearing in the garment of heroism and dedication to the noble cause of saving Israel. The immorality of the war is turned into a legal, respectable, and highly moralistic act.

III

Arab claims or counterclaims—at least those made by the leaders of Arab states and the older generation of Palestinian Arabs—are equally distorted and dishonest. The Arabs argue that they have no alternative but to defend the homeland, to safeguard the integrity of the Arab nation, and to prevent the growth of a foreign agent in their midst which threatens their independence. These arguments are not totally innocent or true. The Arabs in Palestine and outside it were not independent: Their national unity or integrity is little more than a myth or a dream, and their claim to be on the defensive is not true. Furthermore, the Arabs cannot be absolved of the responsibility of acquiescing in the earlier stages of the realization of the idea of a Jewish national home.

At the time when the Zionists chose Palestine as a target for a national home, Palestine and the rest of the Arab world were still dominated by the Turks. Their national status as independent states was as much a dream as the Jewish national home. The area east of the Mediterranean was sparsely populated. Therefore, it seems inaccurate to attack the idea of a Jewish national home in Palestine as an infringement on the political independence of the Arabs at that time. Probably the earliest time at which one might have considered the infringement as real would be the period after World War I, when Turkey was defeated and Arab nationalism seemed to have a chance of succeeding. Even at that time Palestine was singled out by the victorious powers and by the League of Nations to be put under British mandate. All other Arab territories were soon after declared independent or semi-independent, and a monarchial or republican form of goverment was clearly specified. In 1919, the All-Arab Palestinian Conference demanded, among other things, the establishment of a united Syrian government that would consist of Syria, Lebanon, Jordan, and Palestine; no demand for a Palestinian state was made or apparently contemplated. When the State of Israel was established, it was not imposed on an Arab state; it did not reduce the status of any Arab state; it did not prevent the establishment of a Palestinian state, as will be shown in the following chapter. Golda Meir may have overstressed this point when she denied that there was a Palestinian nation, but she was correct in substance. The Palestinian Arab state had not existed yet. It is true that the establishment of the State of Israel reduced the potential territory that might have become a Palestinian state, but this is only a hypothetical and not a real situation. There were no guarantees that the potential territory would not have been populated by other than Arabs in the meantime. Therefore, the Arabs' claim that they were defending their independence cannot be true. At least some of the Arabs undoubtedly were opposed to the Balfour Declaration and were anxious to end the British mandate and establish their own state, but the Jews of Palestine were equally anxious to establish a state of their own. Why should one group feel more entitled to independence than the other is unclear to me, unless one is ready to admit a bias in favor of one group or the other. The Arabs exaggerate the infringement on their political status and rights to independence caused by the creation of a Jewish national home in a part of Palestine.

The Arabs may seem a little more justified in claiming that an Israeli state in Palestine would infringe on their unity as a nation in the sense that that would permit a foreign agent to penetrate in their midst. This argument, however, has little substance. The Arabs may be a nation, but only in the broad terms that the Jews of the world are a nation. They have the same institutions, heritage, language, and religion. However, politically, geographically, socially, and economically, Arab national unity has so far been a myth. Although Islam is the main religion of the Arabs, there are other religions in the area, including Druzism and Christianity. The Moslems themselves are divided into different sects whose antagonism to each other might equal their antagonism to outsiders. Furthermore, religion—Christianity, for example —has not been a viable basis for political unity. The Arabs use one language but its many dialects often make communication in daily life difficult. The major disunity is political. We cannot speak politically of an Arab nation. The North Africans have little in common with Saudi Arabia, Jordan, Iraq, or Syria. Egypt, the center of Arabism, still has many historical and cultural differences from all the other Arab countries. The Arabs might constitute a nation geographically, if there is such a thing, but this is true only as an idea. The Arab countries have been geographically differentiated, and their borders more frequently have been closed to each other than open. How can there be national unity without removing border restrictions on mobility from one region to another? Indeed, that the Arab countries were under the simultaneous domination of three different foreign powers (Britain, France, and Italy) would preclude the pretended unity, although some Arab countries maintained partial independence. Thus, with four sources of political influence acting on the same stage, national unity could hardly be more than a potentiality.

A major blow to the claim of Arab national unity is the economic differentiation among the various regions. Some countries or regions are more favorably endowed than the others, and some have more population pressure relative to their resources than the others. The wealth of Iraq, Libya, and the other oil-rich territories can be a thorn in the heart of Arab unity, unless labor and capital mobility can be guaranteed, as it is in the United States. Egypt, the most populated and powerful of the Arab countries, is also one of the poorest relative to its population. Its power may seem a threat to the wealthier but weaker Arab countries. The potential conflict frequently has come to the surface with tragic results. The idea of an Arab nation was not strong enough to prevent tragedies in Yemen and Jordan and in the relations between Syria and Lebanon and between Iraq and its neighbors. Therefore, to argue that the Arab war against Israel is partly to safeguard national unity seems to be untrue and misleading. Nor does it seem logical to argue that Israel threatens Arab national unity when Iran and Turkey, both neighbors, do not pose that threat. The truth of the matter is that the Arabs wanted to retain the piece of real estate on which Israel chose to build a national home. The Arab national integrity arguments only rationalize a war for territorial possession.

Probably the strongest indictment of the Arabs is the degree of their acquiescence in the establishment of the state of Israel and the fact that they received gains in the process of bargaining with respect to Israel. The Arabs' involvement, cooperation, and silent approval probably date as far back as the early Jewish settlement in Palestine, although they officially only date back to the years preceding the World War I. In the early period of settlement and even after the Balfour Declaration up to 1947, *the Jews acquired land for settlement by purchase from Arab owners.* The Arabs took advantage of the situation and raised the price of land. They sold the land through Arab brokers with full knowledge of the purpose of these transactions. If they had any doubts as to the potential effects of these land transactions, they must have been alleviated by the character of settlement and its paramilitary organization. Settlements grew and towns were built, immigration continued, and it gradually became apparent that the Jewish settlers were forming a government within a government. Yet the sale of land continued. The people who sold land were not starving peasants and small owners; most were wealthy land owners and leaders who pretended to oppose Jewish immigration and settlement. It is beyond any doubt that all settlement up to the establishment of the State of Israel was on land legally acquired from Arabs who had voluntarily sold the land and enjoyed high prices. How can the Arabs then justify the charge that the Jews are intruders, aggressors, and imperialists?

The Palestinian Arabs who sold land were divided among themselves. Big factions were willing to accept the partition of Palestine recommended by the Royal Commission in 1937. Even the White Paper, which would allow Jewish immigration for five years or until it had constituted a third of the total population, was accepted by the Arabs as a victory, although they knew that it would be difficult to stop the implementation of a Jewish national home once that many Jews had settled in the land. Despite their declarations, the Palestinian Arabs were caught unprepared when the time came for a showdown; they had expended little genuine effort to oppose the apparently successful policy for a Jewish state.

Arab responsibility goes beyond individual actions and the sale of land. The responsibility falls on officials and royalty who bargained with Britain for the division of Arab land after its liberation from Turkey. King Hussein the First, his son King Abdullah, and even the present King Hussein are said to have been in collaboration with Britain and with Jewish leaders. The then Amir Abdullah is said to have favored partition as recommended by the 1937 Royal Commission. As king, shortly after the War of 1948, Abdullah negotiated with Golda Meir and ceded a strip of land along the border to Israel, hoping for concessions he never realized. Before the overthrow of the Hashemite dynasty, Iraqi leaders were equally involved in the negotiations with Britain and the leaders of Zionism. King Feisal of Iraq signed an agreement with Haim Weizmann in 1919 in support of the Balfour Declaration. Some argue that these leaders actually had no choice in the matter since Britain already had planned the creation of a Jewish national home. Even if this were true, how can those Arab leaders justify cooperation with Britain and then turn around and prolong a war which is costing men and material and still blame the whole thing on others?

The responsibility of the Arab countries in failing to prevent the establishment of Israel, and their apparent cooperation can probably be illustrated best by looking into the actual wars that have taken place. It is well known that in 1948 the Jordanian forces withdrew from upper Galilee, Safad, and Tiberius, even though they were in control of the whole region. The Iraqi forces have always been within reach of the battlefield but have taken no part in repelling Jewish forces. The Syrians, Lebanese, and even the Egyptians did a lot of talking but little active defending up to, and during, the 1947–1948 war. The Arabs of North Africa and of the Peninsula were virtually neutral to all action until then; they since have contributed some material aid and a lot of talk. Whether they could have changed the history of Palestine is uncertain, but there is little evidence that they really cared enough to try or to evaluate the situation seriously. In fact, there is a possibility that the Arab leaders did not care enough and therefore were willing to leave the high command of the Arab forces to King Abdullah of Jordan, who was collaborating with the British and Zionist leaders. In turn, King Abdullah was responsible for helping to create an atmosphere of panic, fear, and even hopelessness among the

Palestinians in order that they would flee their homes and make room for the new state of Israel. His reward would be the acquisition of that part of Palestine which would remain outside the borders of Israel. In other words, it is highly reasonable to believe that King Abdullah had agreed to the partition of Palestine and had arranged to realize the plan by instigating the movement of people and by annexing the eastern part of Palestine. Other Arab leaders either acquiesced or did not know or care about what was happening. Thus, Israel was established, Jordan acquired additional territory, and the people of Palestine have suffered the results. How can the Arabs blame these results on someone else when the immorality of the actions of their own leaders and their responsibility for the war are so obvious?

The various Arab armies not only failed to help the Palestinians, but they also failed to cooperate with each other sufficiently to prevent the disasters suffered by Egypt in 1956 and by both Jordan and Egypt in 1967. As far back as the 1936 rebellion of the Palestinians against the British, the surrounding Arab countries gave only half-hearted support. Their leadership, equipment, and organization was inadequate, although Jews all over the world were helping the Jewish cause. It is true that they were under the influence of foreign governments, and therefore their actions might have been restricted, but their aid in 1947 and after they became fully independent was not more than it was before. The Palestinians continued to be poorly organized, equipped, and led. I remember that I went on guard duty against the impending danger of an invasion by the Haganah forces, armed with a pistol and six bullets; others carried shotguns; some were armed with sticks. The Israelis were coming with tanks and planes. Where were the Arab leaders and where was the help of the Arab countries, most of which were already independent!

And yet, the Arab leaders would not leave the Palestinians alone. They formed what seemed to be a unified force to replace the British as soon as the Mandate came to an end. The Palestinians were encouraged to leave their homes with the promise that they soon would all be able to come back triumphantly. The leaders of the Arab countries broadcasted great and patriotic messages from all directions, but few were ready to engage the enemy. The fully equipped Iraqis were at Ras-al-Iyn and could have helped a great deal, but they stood aloof. The Jordanian army engaged the enemy in certain areas but withdrew from others, even when there was little necessity to withdraw. The Egyptians occupied Gaza and its surroundings, but that was to an extent consistent with the plan for an Israeli state. Other Arab countries did little to help the Palestinians in their presumably Arab struggle.

The Arab disgrace and lack of cooperation have probably been displayed best in the treatment of Arab refugees. Jordan acquired the eastern part of Palestine and imposed Jordanian citizenship on the people—just as Israel imposed its citizenship on the Arabs who stayed in the area occupied by Israel. In all the other Arab countries the vast majority of Palestinians have been treated as outsiders; they have been precluded from citizenship, ownership of property, and most professional and even nonprofessional occupations, and have been held in refugee camps. Many reasons have been given for this treatment, but in fact, the Arab countries were not willing to let the Palestinians share the economic opportunities of these countries. Narrow Syrian, Lebanese, or Egyptian nationalism, rather than Arab nationalism, prevailed; the Palestinians were treated as outsiders. Yet, the Arab countries go on fanning the fire of war in the name of helping these same Palestinians. How dishonest and misleading! Dishonesty has continued even after the first generation of Arab leaders involved in the conflict has passed away. The immorality of Arab insistence on the war is glaringly clear and yet it goes on.

The immorality of the war has been observed and noted by President Bourguiba of Tunisia. In 1965 he pointed out the misleading attitude of Arab leaders who insisted on war; he confessed, and has been proved correct, that a war against Israel would be difficult to win, that the use of Palestine as a means of sustaining an artificial and false unity among the Arabs was dishonest, and that the problem of Palestine should be handled by the Palestinians, just as the Algerians and Tunisians have handled their own problems. In spite of these declarations the Arab leaders have continued to insist on a warlike and hateful approach, have given little consideration to the Palestinian Arabs, and have failed to achieve any success on behalf of the suffering refugees.

It is true that since 1956, and more so since 1967, the Arab countries have no longer fought a Palestinian war or for a Palestinian cause. They have been fighting their own war and for their own cause but in the name of Arab Palestine. Egypt, Jordan, and Syria have lost territory and are trying to regain it, but the cause is said to be Palestinian. Needless to say, the Palestinians have discovered these distortions and have begun to take matters in their own hands. Since then Jordanians and Palestinians have shed Arab blood. The alleged Arab unity and sameness of purpose have been forgotten. By their divisiveness the Jordanians and the Palestinians have contributed to the full realization of Israeli triumphs. In the meantime, hundreds of thousands of Palestinians remain in refugee camps, in poverty, and in uncertainty of the future.

The battle for a small territory has turned into a perennial conflict between two Semitic peoples and between segments of the Arab world because of the failure of the leaders of both groups to face the facts with honesty, realism, and humane consideration of each other. The impact will be felt more bitterly when this generation of refugee-camp children grows into adulthood and seeks revenge and destruction against the "villains," whether Arabs or Jews.

IV

The immorality of the Middle Eastern War frequently has been reinforced by the actions of foreign powers, most of whom are motivated by self-interest, guilt feelings, and imperialistic tendencies. The early Zionist ideas were accepted gradually by Britain, France, and the United States. By World War I, many countries were sold on the idea of a national home for the Jews in Palestine. Why was it so? Had these people no reverence for the rights of the Arabs who inhabited the land? How did they go about supporting the Zionist movement? Several factors enter into this discussion: There was a great deal of miscalculation regarding Arab opposition and the degree of dislocation that would ensue. At the same time, western nations were planning to replace Turkey as the power in the Middle East. They saw in aid to the Jews in Palestine a way of penetrating the region. This attitude was undoubtedly strengthened by the propaganda and influence of Jewish citizens of Britain, France, the United States, and Russia. The Gentiles probably reinforced the idea of a Jewish national home in order to get rid of Jews in their own countries who might be willing to emigrate. By the time of Hitler's pogroms against the Jews, the western peoples had developed such feelings of guilt for allowing Jews to be inhumanely annihilated that they were willing to aid the cause of Israel extensively, especially aid that entailed no territorial concessions on their part. To bring these plans to fruition, the western powers used international parleys, bargained with the Arabs, extended financial and technical aid to the Jewish movement, supplied the necessary arms and espionage, and put the seal of international respectability on the Israeli claims by voting for the creation of the State of Israel in the United Nations. Foreign support for Israel has continued but has been tied in with the cold war and the conflict between East and West and between the superpowers. The rationale of the early years has now been replaced by irrational fear and the cold war. The war goes on, immoral as it is, and the Palestinians continue to suffer the consequences. And as if to complicate matters further, these powers have persisted in voting for the rehabilitation and repatriation of the Palestinian Arabs with full knowledge that such a solution is impractical and, in fact, dishonest. Let us look at some details to illustrate these points.

It would be an oversimplification to suggest that the foreign powers had wanted the course of events in the Middle East to turn the way it has insofar as the dislocation of people is concerned. There is little doubt that these powers have miscalculated in that the conflict has gone on for so long and in that antagonism and hatred have become deeply imbedded. They had looked forward to replacing Turkey in the Arab lands. They met cooperation from Arab leaders, and they had the upper hand in the region as soon as Turkey was defeated. They had reasons to believe that their plan could be implemented with much less cost than has been the case. There is also little doubt that until 1940 their plan was working. Persecution of the Jews in World War II added urgency for its implementation. Jewish suffering in Europe was probably a major factor in precluding gradual implemention, arousing antagonism, and causing the eruption of a violent and brutal conflict, contrary to earlier expectations. It is also doubtful that these foreign powers expected the Arabs to flee the land as quickly as they did, or that the Israeli forces would make as many gains in such a short time. In fact, such gains were not apparent until the cease-fire, which took place in 1948. The ceasefire was opportune for the Israelis since they were able to secure arms from Czechoslovakia and reorganize themselves for more fighting. The foreign powers did not expect Israel to be so successful in defeating the Egyptians in 1956 and probably in 1967. Thus, while they had planned the creation of a Jewish national home in Palestine, they were not prepared for the tragic effects suffered by hundreds of thousands of innocent people.

The policies of the foreign powers were strengthened by internal forces within those countries, which made aid to Zionism an attractive national policy. Among these forces were the influential Jewish groups which contributed to Jewish ideals and persuaded their governments to extend the necessary aid. Jewish forces in Britain were probably more responsible than any other such communities in influencing policy in the early years, as shown by the Balfour Declaration. French elements were probably less influential, in part because of the instability of political forces in France and the difficulty of building a dependable structure to aid the Jewish cause. Nevertheless, France more often than not has been a strong ally of Israel. In fact, for a long period of time after the establishment of Israel, France was the main source of arms and equipment, including the planes that won the 1956 and 1967 wars. However, since 1948 the most influential Jewish community has been the American group. They have managed to commit the U. S. policy to a guarantee of Israeli security; they have financed the development of Israel; and they have secured a disproportionately favorable attitude of the non-Jewish Americans toward Israel. Propaganda and finance, as well as the power of their vote in state and local politics, were used effectively to serve the welfare of Israel and its political interests.

It is significant that the impact of these forces has been so strong that public opinion and the leaders of the major American political parties have been blinded to the immorality of the war, the distortions embodied in the Zionist and Israeli agruments, and the misrepresentation of the Arab cause. Most Americans are poorly informed of the facts and history of the conflict. They have been convinced that helping Israel is simply a humane act of rescuing innocent people from a cruel policy of annihilation practiced by the Arabs. They do not know who is on the defense and who is on the offense. They have been blind to the immorality of the conflict as it has developed over the last half century. By adding their weight to a faulty and immoral policy, they have allowed such misguided policies to snowball in the cause of one people against another without intending the results to be what they have been. The western governments, in order to secure votes, have concurred and permitted that trend to become an integral feature of their policies toward the war in the Middle East.

Both the miscalculation and the bias in the western world have been supported to a certain extent by feelings of guilt on the part of these powers. The guilt has been caused by awareness of the discriminatory practices against Jews in most of the western Christian countries for many centuries; it also has resulted from failure to rescue the Jews from persecution in Nazi Germany before millions had been annihilated. And as if to atone for these failures and in order to correct injustices, they have been quite receptive to Zionist propaganda and have been easily persuaded that the tragedy suffered by the Arabs has been exaggerated. Unfortunately, both sources of guilt feelings have persisted, and the western powers are doing little to amend the situation within their own countries. We still hear of anti-Jewish and anti-Semitic practices in virtually all the western countries. We also hear of little serious effort to combat the alleged anti-Semitism in

Soviet Russia, or at least to ascertain the truth of these allegations. In other words, there is a high degree of hypocrisy in the policy to aid Israel as a way of combatting anti-Semitism, when present practices are equally discriminatory and possibly anti-Semitic. This same story has been repeated many times during the past ten centuries, but few are able to see that the western powers are trying to correct one immoral set of practices against Jews by aiding and developing an equally immoral set of practices against Arabs.

These policies have been enhanced by the fact that their implementation relieved the western powers of any obligation to open their own gates to Jewish immigrants from places in which they were persecuted. They also relieved any obligation to surrender territory for a Jewish national home. Canada and the United States could have offered to welcome Jewish immigration on a large scale and might have set aside a separate area for a Jewish national home. But why do so if Palestine could be secured and designated as the Jewish national home! Indeed, aid to a Jewish cause in Palestine might even rid these western powers of some Jewish elements without appearing as anti-Semitism. Without openly declaring such intentions, the idea of Palestine as the site was adopted and the cause of Israel was widely patronized.

Not only were these policies hidden behind a screen of goodness and humaneness, but they also were rationalized by an apparent agreement between western powers and certain Arab leaders. The British and, later, the United States authorities bargained with Sherif Hussein (later king), his sons Feisal and King Abdullah, and with other Arab leaders. For all practical purposes these policies seemed acceptable to the Arabs who were awarded certain benefits in return. Indeed, the benefits were received before and after the establishment of the state of Israel. The Arabs were aided in their revolt against Turkey; some were made kings; others received riches, concessions, and protection. As a result the western powers could easily point to these agreements and convey the impression that their policies were acceptable to the Arabs. The people in general had little reason to doubt the validity of such announcements. Thus, while the people were being misled, the opposition of the Arabs was being overshadowed until open war broke out and the Arabs were branded as aggressors, in which case they lost more public support than they had had before.

The western powers have contributed materially and politically to the realization of the Jewish national home. However, to render the defense of the Jewish cause legitimate and respectable, they sponsored that cause in international parleys, in international diplomacy, and finally voted for the creation of the State of Israel in the United Nations. Once the State of Israel had been created, aid to Israel became diplomatically acceptable and could be used as a whip against the Arab countries. This was the beginning of the division of the Middle Eastern countries between East and West. Although the United States and Soviet Russia had long wished to set foot in the Middle East, and Britain and France were sorry to leave the region after independence of the different countries became imminent, the conflict between Israel and the Arab nations was a natural means for the newcomers to become involved and for the departing countries to keep some interest in the area. The cold war found fertile soil in the Middle East. The United States supported Israel without equivocation while they frowned upon aid to the Arabs. The Soviets were watching and ready, and the Arabs took advantage. And thus the dirty game of risking other peoples' interests came into being in the Middle East. The Soviet Union defends the Arabs against imperialism; the United States defends Israel as a humane act and in support of national independence. Behind all this is the simple fact that both superpowers are serving only their own interests; the Arab nations and Israel are tools in the cold war, regardless of the degree of independence they pretend to have. In fact, without the outside aid and the so-called balance of power policy or armament neither party would be able to continue this war, to defend itself as it has, or to boast of its independence and power. The tragic thing is that cold-war diplomacy, which obviously is preferable to a hot active war, does not apply in the Middle East. The war in the Middle East is already hot; more than a million people have been dislocated; many more are living in a state of tension, insecurity, and constant danger of being a war casualty. And yet these superpowers continue cold-war diplomacy in the region. As will be shown below, this involvement has been a serious obstacle in peacemaking in the region. Furthermore, the rationale of aid to rescue Jews in the early period has now been replaced by a cold-war rationale which forces people into one camp or the other and makes the arms race a way of life. The immorality of the war is thus termed an indispensible fight for survival in the face of danger from the other camp. The Arabs and Israelis are in danger of losing the ability to resolve that conflict on their own since the conflict has become a part of the cold war to which the superpowers are parties.

The cold war and the alleged friendship with one group or the other have been integrated with business interests in the West and their partners in the Middle East. For example, the oil interests would like the western powers to stay in the area at all costs to protect them. The armament industry would like to make sure that they are able to sell outdated equipment and surplus weapons. It has been suggested that the United States delivers arms to Israel for testing, just as the Soviets have tested the effectiveness of the SAMs II and III in Egypt against the American weapons used by the Israelis. Thus the business interests and the military establishment in both East and West have taken advantage of the conflict to create a laboratory for their weapons, regardless of the destructive impact of these weapons to peacemaking efforts and to men and material in the region.

In summary, it appears that the foreign powers have supported the war and the conflict between Arabs and Israelis as an integral part of their imperialistic policies. They have involved the Middle East in the cold war and succeeded in dividing those countries between the two camps, East and West. The western powers have supported and aided the cause of Israel with little concern for the negative impact on the Arabs. The Soviets and the Chinese are supporting the Arabs only to spite the western powers. Both East and West allowed expediency to provide the rationale for sustaining and possibly prolonging an immoral war. The question remains whether alternative and more efficient methods, other than war, could have been found to realize the same objectives. This question will be answered affirmatively in the last chapter. However, it should be noted that the war itself can hardly be justified even on utilitarian basis since the war cannot be won by either side. Indeed some of the war methods used tended to create insecurity, hate, and prolonged antagonism without bringing about any real gains to offset these high costs.

V

In spite of the restraint often noted on both Arab and Israeli sides, there have been occasions which are a disgrace to both sides. For example, both Arab and Jewish civilian communities have been completely disrupted in the name of independence: homes have been blown out; innocent people have been killed; terror has been wide-spread, and industrial and agricultural production has been interrupted. What are the gains? Israel has won land and a large Arab population, which spells out big headaches and insecurity. It has also accumulated enemies within and without the Middle East. The Arabs have lost land, people, and capital. They have apparently given up many of the original causes for which they fought. Now they seem anxious only to recover territory lost in the 1967 war. Even if they secure any gains, these would only reduce the losses already suffered. In the meantime, the Arabs have exposed their weaknesses, displayed their lack of unity, and shed each other's blood. Jealousy and distrust between one Arab country and another, and between one Arab leader and another, have been aggravated by the Arab-Israeli war. The extreme of this enmity in the last three years has been reflected in the bloody conflict between the Palestinian Arabs and King Hussein of Jordan. The inter-Arab war has added to the immorality of the total war, as more innocent people are being dislocated, killed, or jailed in the name of justice, independence, and sovereignty.

The hate and distrust between Arabs and Jews and among Arabs have in part resulted from the behavior of the antagonistic parties in the war. I have in mind individual acts by both sides which only could generate hate and move the two parties further apart. Acts of terrorism have been common and have helped to lengthen the war, to reduce the chances for peace, and in some instances, to give added support to the mutual distrust between the warring parties. There is little reason to trace these acts to the prestatehood days. Until then fighting was presumably done by guerrillas and therefore would not be subject to the present indictment. Acts of terrorism by organized armies or with the aid of regular armies are the kind of behavior intended in this argument.

The Arabs have justifiably condemned the Israelis for acts of terror against innocent civilians more than once. Probably the classic examples are those of Quluniya and Deir Yasseen. The killing of Count Bernadotte, a peacemaker, is another. The evacuation and demolition of numerous villages and homes are others. Israel has recently banished Arab families from Gaza to the Sinai desert and placed them in a concentration camp.

The Arabs have been equally cruel and unprincipled, a recent example being the decapitation of an Israeli tractor driver. The organized Arab armies have not had many chances to undertake such acts against the Israelis. They have committed acts of terror either against Jews in the Arab countries or by aiding the Palestinian guerrillas in their terrorist acts against the Israelis. Shelling of settlements and schools and the attacks on school buses are simply acts of terror.

Acts of terrorism and irregular warfare have obviously been intended to strike fear in the heart of the opponent. Frequently the short-term objectives have been successfully achieved, but the greater and more permanent objectives of a settlement or a victory have been pushed further into the future. One might equally condemn the acts of terrorism by the Palestinian guerrillas, although such acts are predictable and therefore less shocking, even if not more justifiable. However, when aided by the regular armies of the Arab countries, these acts become equally immoral and contribute to the failure of peacemaking.

VI

So far I have touched only on the nonmaterial effects or implications of the war and why the war should be branded immoral. But there is no reason why the material effects should be left out. The economic costs of the war and the waste of resources resulting from it are strong moral arguments against the war. Given the underdevelopment of the region, the poverty of the people, and the pressure of increasing population on the local resources, it seems immoral for any government to use resources on war at the expense of immediate demands for daily life of the people. Indeed, one may brand all war expenditure as a waste and as immoral with the possible exception of the one situation in which the mere survival of a nation is at stake and its borders are actually invaded. Even this kind of war expenditure may be a justifiable exception only if other less costly alternatives are not available.

Needless to say, both the Arabs and Israel claim that they are at war only to defend their mere existence and their legal boundaries. Although the nature of the war has changed and what began as a defense may have turned into an offense, it is doubtful that after 1948 the war has always been defensive. It is equally doubtful that no alternative safeguard for existence and security has existed. The main problem is that the objectives have changed and what would have been regarded as offensive now can be reclassified as defensive. For example, the moving borders of Israel have changed the character of the war in the Sinai or near the Suez Canal from offensive to what is now called defensive. The Arabs threaten action to free areas which might not have been occupied had they not invaded Israel in 1947. Furthermore, it would be hard to accept the idea that there was, and is, no alternative to war. The mere willingness of either or both parties to search for alternatives suggests that such alternatives do exist. To that extent, therefore, all expenditures that go beyond the "normal" needs for security of the borders and internal security in times of peace should be regarded as wasteful and unnecessary expenditure. And to the extent that such expenditure is undertaken at the expense of humanitarian and welfare benefits, it should be branded immoral. The immorality becomes glaringly clear when we note the magnitude of these expenditures and economic losses relative to the prevailing economic conditions.

To compute the cost of the war between Israel and the Arabs, one should take into consideration both the hot- and the cold-war costs and should include the loss of human capital through death, handicap, and dislocation and imposed idleness. One should also include the destruction of fixed capital including public and private assets. Finally, one should consider the direct expenditure on war and defense over and above what would be expended in peacetime. These costs are difficult, if not impossible, to compute. For our purposes it is sufficient to make rough estimates which would show the magnitude of the material losses contingent on failing to arrive at a peaceful solution of the conflict. Let us look at some of the losses of income because of the dislocation of people. (I shall be very conservative in these estimates to avoid an exaggerated bias.) About 750,000 Palestinians, on the average, have been on the refugee lists of the United Nations for a period of more than 20 years. If we assume a loss of income of $50 per capita per year for 20 years, the loss would be $750 million. Another 250,000 people have been dislocated in Egypt and Syria for about four years, adding another $50 million; the loss will continue at a minimum of $40 million per year as long as these people are considered refugees and dislocated. Another direct loss of income was inflicted on Egypt by the destruction of oil refineries and the closure of the Suez Canal, at a cost of about $200 million per year, or of more than $1 billion up to this time. The loss of human capital through death on the front, handicap, or mobilization is hard to estimate because of the lack of precise data. Some estimates, for example, put Arab losses at about 50,000 people, while Israeli losses were about 2,000 dead and wounded. It is equally difficult to estimate the losses due to physical destruction of homes and other buildings. Many villages have been totally erased and towns in the canal area completely destroyed and made uninhabitable. If we were to estimate a $500 loss per dislocated person for property destruction, the loss would be at least $500 million. The cost of not using the Suez Canal is almost a third of the transportation cost which the consumer of oil in Europe has to pay. Finally, we have the direct cost of the war, as represented by the defense budget of each country over and above the peacetime defense budget. Put together, Egypt, Syria, Iraq, Jordan, and Israel have spent more than $5 billion between 1950 and 1970. Thus, if we estimate the economic losses and waste generated by the failure to arrive at peace, the most conservative figure would be close to $10 billion, or more than the cost of ten High Aswan Dams. Obviously, this is only one fourth of the money the United States spends in one year on the war in Vietnam. But by comparison with the living standards in the Middle East and the high scarcity of capital, the loss in the Middle East is far more strategic and immoral than the waste incurred by the United States on the war in Vietnam.

It may be ironic that we should regard the expenditure on war in the Middle East as a cost to the people of that region when a large part of that expenditure is recovered from the outside. My research suggests that the operating costs of the war largely have been replaced by friends and allies of the warring parties to the extent of eliminating the impact of the war on the respective economies. In fact, one can argue that: (1) The war has had such little impact on the per capita disposable income of the warring parties, except that of the Palestinians, that the living standard has not been depressed seriously. The extra burdens caused by the war have been offset by economic growth, foreign aid, or both. (2) The development of the economy on either side has not suffered any serious setbacks and, in some cases, might have benefited from the technological and entrepreneurial impact of the war. With few exceptions, the process of production has not been interrupted in any major industry or strategic sector of the economy to any detrimental extent. (3) The parties to the conflict have had access to resources *to finance the war and to replace the losses.* Indeed, replacement capital has always seemed available, on time, and usable to purchase equipment. Although both sides, at least since 1956, have tried to impress on each other the necessity of compromising and reaching an acceptable settlement, both have found it possible and economically feasible to continue the war, thanks to foreign contributions. To illustrate, the costs of the war to Jordan, over and above the "normal" expenditure of 4 percent of the gross national product for defense, have been estimated at $353.4 million in constant dollars between 1955 and 1964.[2] A rough estimate of the aid received in the same period from the United States alone is $432 million. Adding the aid from the United Kingdom and another $40 million a year from the oil-rich Arab countries, it becomes clear that the was has caused no significant economic burden to Jordan. It is even doubtful that these funds would have been received had there been no war or that the expenditures on war would have been put to more productive uses. Furthermore, aid has been forthcoming in such a way as to replace losses and defray costs as they arise so that the government of Jordan would be under no undue economic pressure to stop the war. The replacement of military equipment and other war losses has made it especially easy to continue to war.

[2]Nadav Safran, *From War to War* (New York: Western Publishing Co. 1969) p. 197.

The costs of the war to Syria, over and above a normal defense expenditure of 4 percent of the gross national product, have been estimated at $429.3 million in constant dollars.[3] Although aid from the United States has been limited (less than $100 million in the last two decades), Syria received about $400 million in military aid from the socialist countries between 1954 and 1967. It received another $460 million, described as economic aid, from the same sources between 1955 and 1967. While the average annual cost of the war was about $42 million, the aid received was close to $70 million. In terms of expenditures and receipts, Syria has had an incentive to sustain tension and continue a war of attrition with Israel.

Egypt's estimated expenditures on account of the war are about $1.3 billion between 1955 and 1964, compared with Israel's estimated expenditure of $896 million in the same period. However, a rough estimate of the foreign aid in loans and grants received by Egypt shows that the United States contributed about a billion dollars in that period. The communist countries contributed about $1.6 billion in military aid between 1954 and 1967 and another $1,679 million in what is classified as economic aid.[4] Russian military aid since 1967 has been estimated between three and four billion dollars, including weapons that are handled by Russians.[5] Assistance from the Arab countries has been sufficient at least to replace the loss of income incurred by closure of the Suez Canal.

[3] *Ibid*, p. 197.

[4] Vassil Vassilev, *Policy in the Soviet Bloc on Aid to Developing Countries* (Paris: Development Center of Organization For Economic Cooperation and Development, 1969), p. 66.

[5] Edward R. F. Sheehan, "The Way Egyptians See Israel, Uncle Sam, the SAM'S," *New York Times Magazine*, Sept. 20, 1970.

Israel has been aided as generously. Rough estimates show that direct aid from the United States was close to half a billion dollars between 1955 and 1964. In addition, Israel received about $200 million from West Germany in that period, over and above the reparation payments of more than $800 million. This aid does not include the extensive help received from the sale of bonds and from contributions by individuals throughout the United States and Europe. Aid from world Jews has been increasing, especially since 1967. Israel is asking for contributions at least equal to the total budget expenditures on war and defense.

Does the fact that war expenditures are covered by receipts from the outside lessen the degree of immorality inherent in this wasteful expenditure? Not at all. Those foreign powers which sustain the war, with all its tragic effects, also share in the responsibility for the continuation of an immoral war. Had they not replaced all or most of these expenditures, Israel and the Arab countries might have looked more seriously for less costly and probably less immoral alternatives. This point may be stressed even further by noting that some of those countries extending aid are themselves short of capital. China sends military aid when the standard of living of the Chinese is one of the lowest in the world. Soviet Russia pours military aid into Egypt, Syria, and Iraq while there are many essential needs still to be satisfied for the Soviet people. Even the United States can make better use of the money spent on the war in the Middle East by clearing the slums or by feeding the starving people all over the world. The immediate results of the military aid is part of the immorality under criticism.

The responsibility of foreign countries for the immoral consequences of the war in the Middle East derives not only from military aid as such, but also the form it takes, the types of weapons provided, and the ease with which weapons are supplied. Probably one of the most important facts about this war is the ability of the warring parties to replace the lost equipment and war material so easily and of technology that seems adequately threatening to sustain the war. Thus the warring parties are able to race with each other as to who has the more advanced weapons, regardless of previous losses. The arms-producing countries have welcomed, and in some cases encouraged, requests for arms deliveries to the Middle East countries. These powers have argued that "military aid and sales programmes directly benefit their own security, provide a lucrative source of income, win economic and political influence, stabilize the balance of power in a given area, spread the increasing capital costs of their own military equipment programmes, or work towards the standardization of equipment, communications and procedures throughout alliance structures."[6] Consequently, the Middle Eastern countries often have been armed far beyond their capacities to use the arms they received. It has become a matter of prestige for them to acquire modern equipment. However, the arms race has been significantly reinforced by the balance of power concept pursued by the arms producing countries. Thus, no sooner had Egypt lost its air power than the Soviet Union was ready to replace everything. Similarly, as soon as Israel began to lose planes, the United States started to deliver them in order to restore a balance of power allegedly disturbed during the current ceasefire. Neither country has faced a short-

---

[6]John L. Sutton and Geoffrey Kemp, *Arms to Developing Countries, 1945–1965*, Adelphi Papers, no. 28 (London: The Institute for Strategic Studies, 1966).

age of arms, even when they could not afford to pay for them. No doubt the ease of replacement of weapons has been one of the major contributors to the continuation of war. The justifications are many, but few can escape the brand of immorality once the possible alternatives and the losses so far incurred are explored.

| Futility of Peacemaking
in the Middle East

I

In 1958, I had a friendly debate with an American about the Arab-Israeli conflict. The debate lasted for many hours, spread over a number of days, after which I wrote down my recollections. I am reproducing tEM AS I recorded them, with only minor editorial changes.

AN ISRAELI CITIZEN ON THE DEFENSE

"And what is the future of the State of Israel in the midst of a hostile Arab world?" asked my companion, while we were driving alongside the beautiful orange groves of Southern California, which, more than ever before, made me long for home.

"The State is there to stay," I answered with certainty and confidence.

Without hesitation, my companion retorted: "That I have heard and read very often, but can you really live without making peace with your neighbors, if only for economic and security purposes?" I tried to convince him that we are ready to make peace with any or all the Arab countries and are willing to meet with them at any time or place. I reminded him that David Ben-Gurion had as recently as July 29 of this year expressed in the *Knesset* (the Israeli Parliament) the readiness of Israel to conclude peace with her Arab neighbors at any time they so wished. My companion, however, was not easily persuaded by what he considered "flattering" words or "phony" announcements, for he emphatically contradicted; *"What exactly have you Israelis done to promote peace with the Arab countries?"* After a moment of deep thinking I, for the first time, wished that he had addressed his question to Ben-Gurion.

My companion was an American who has a great interest in international affairs, particularly with the problems of the Near East; consequently, he had followed events there very closely. He pointed out three main problems that should be solved before peace between the Arab countries and Israel could be concluded: (1) the Arab refugee problem; (2) the borders between Israel and her Arab neighbors; and (3) the acceptance of Israel as a Near Eastern nation by the Arab people, the point which he regarded as the most important.

It is interesting to observe that my companion constantly stressed the fact that the Arabs had always been the losers in the Palestine question in particular and in their relation to Israel in general. He felt that any approach to the above three problems should be oriented to the peculiar position in which the Arabs have found themselves. Any solution to be suggested should provide a premise according to which these Arabs could be redressed and compensated not only materially but also and primarily for the moral loss they had suffered.

"I am afraid that you are biased in favor of the Arabs," I

said later when we talked politics again. "Take the refugees, for instance, why do the Arab countries not have them settled on their vast underpopulated territories in Syria and Iraq, especially the latter from which many thousands of Jews have been evacuated and absorbed in Israel? We have always been willing to carry our responsibility toward the refugees within the framework of a general solution to the problem and have said so. Why do not the Arabs carry their share of that responsibility?" But again I failed to win the argument as my companion reminded me that these Arab refugees had evacuated their homes in Palestine unwillingly and that war effects cannot become permanent conditions on de facto basis. He also reminded me that the Arab refugees have the right to go back to their homes on the basis of U.N. Resolution 194 of 1948, which was reiterated in 1951 and ever since. "Furthermore," he added, "can you not appreciate the emotional attachment of these refugees to their homes in which they have lived for centuries? It is amazing how the Jewish people still feel an attachment to Palestine from which they have been away for two thousand years, yet they deny the same rights to the Arabs? Even if you maintain that your relationship to Palestine is based on religious factors you will still be unable to exclude the Arabs from their homes if only for the same reasons which are sacred to you; and if you think you could, then you would be challenging the basic doctrines of both Christianity and Islam!"

I felt, no doubt, that my companion was justified in appreciating the importance of the refugees' problem from the legal as well as the moral standpoints. But, to my satisfaction, he did not fail to appreciate the difficulties involved in repatriating the Arab refugees to their homes in Israel, at least from the physical aspect, since most of their homes and lands have been occupied by Jewish immigrants. He would not accept the argument that their repatriation would constitute a security problem for the the State of Israel. It was his conviction that once the refugees were satisfied, they would no longer have a reason to oppose the State. Nevertheless, he indirectly took account of this problem when I asked him what solution he had in mind that would be practical and generally acceptable to both the Arabs and Israel. "First," he said, "Israel should recognize the legal and moral rights of the refugees to be repatriated. Once this is done, in compliance with the U.N. Resolution, two alternatives may be suggested: The first is to allow the refugees to come back to their homes if they wish to—I do not think many of them care to —or be resettled permanently, with compensation in either case, in the Arab countries. The second alternative is to allow them to set up an independent state in the eastern part of Palestine and then let them decide their policy concerning their own neighbors." In either case it was clear that the refugees themselves were to be allowed the freedom of choice as a moral rehabilitation and as a means of pacification which would diminish their menace to Israel. The second alternative, which was more appealing to me, certainly introduced another major problem which my companion had mentioned at the beginning of our discussions, namely, the border question.

"This seems to have become a classical question," I pointed out. "Whenever you talk with anyone about the problem of Palestine he at once mentions the borders. I know what you have in mind; you mean that we should go back to the United Nations Partition plan of 1947 and give up the extra territory which we hold at present."

"Exactly," he promptly answered, adding, "and there is no reason why this extra territory, which is about one-third of your country, should remain with you contrary to the United Nations Plan, by virtue of which you exist as a state. Furthermore, the United Nations has not invalidated that Plan and it cannot, therefore, be a 'dead letter' as your leaders claim it to be. De facto borders based on force cannot be permanent borders; and, if you claim that your present position concerning the borders is justified, why have you not persuaded the United Nations to cancel their above-mentioned resolutions and thus disarm the Arabs of an international document with which they politically and morally fight you?" As if knowing what was going on in my mind, he added that should Israel claim that armies of occupation withdraw only after war comes to an end and that the war with the Arabs has not actually ended—since there is only a truce with them—would it mean that we will withdraw back to the Partition Plan borders whenever peace is concluded? I withheld my answer, recalling that in the *Knesset* meeting mentioned above the prime minister affirmed the contrary, even were the recommendations to modify the borders to come from a summit conference.

A more interesting discussion, however, took place when we considered the third major point relating to the acceptance of Israel by the Arabs. Thinking that that was "my day," I reminded him of the negative attitude that the Arabs have maintained towards Israel and how consistently they have expressed their determination to eliminate the State of Israel from existence. I reminded him also of the continuous attacks on the border settlements, the refusal of the Arabs even to sit with Israeli leaders to negotiate a solution, and finally of the economic boycott they have imposed on Israel. But, to my dismay, my companion again countered with the question: "What concretely have you done about this negative attitude? Have you done anything other than using force or identifying yourselves with the target of Arab and Near Eastern nationalism? Have you really attempted to prove your identity as a Near Eastern nation, or have you for once tried to identify yourselves with the people of the Near East in their struggle to achieve independence and overcome colonialism?" Even there I found his argument justified. Why has Israel not identified itself with the peoples of Cyprus and Algeria, or why has it not supported, morally at least, Arab nationalism and longing to rid themselves of archaic monarchies in the service of imperialism? Certainly Israel did make such an attempt by congratulating Sudan upon the occasion of its independence, but who would fail to see that these congratulations, which were ignored by the Sudanese, were more an attempt to isolate Sudan from the family of Arab nations?

This argument reminded me of a talk I gave to a Jewish community in the United States, in which I emphasized the need for Israel to identify itself with the forces against imperialism in the Near East. On that occasion my audience was greatly opposed to my views, arguing that Israel is nothing more than a puppet of the United States, Britain, and France and, therefore, cannot sever its friendship with their governments. Then, I thought that the dream of Winston Churchill must have come true, as he expressed it in 1920 when he said: "If, as may well happen, there should be created in our lifetime by the banks of Jordan a Jewish State under the protection of the British Crown which might comprise three or four millions of Jews, an event will have occurred in the history of the world which would from every point of view be beneficial, and would be especially in harmony with the interests of the British Empire." The Empire is crumbling but the State is there. How true is my companion's view that to survive every organism has to adjust itself to the environment as well as to try to modify that environment; the same applies to the State of Israel. Identification with the Near East community is an adjustment which is indispensable for peaceful coexistence with the Arabs.

The climax to our discussions was reached when my companion found out that I am an Arab, although a citizen of Israel, and asked the usual question of how the Arabs in Israel were treated. I explained that certain things were good while others were bad, reminding my companion of the Israeli government's apprehensions toward its Arab citizens under the prevailing political circumstances. I also mentioned specifically the progress that had been achieved in the field of education among the Arabs in Israel, at least in terms of the number of students that have access to education. But, to my surprise, he proved to be very well-informed of the conditions there. He asked, "Why is there military government in the sectors inhabited by Arabs, and how many villages have been helped to install electricity and running water? Why are the Arab workers not accepted in the *Histadrut* (General Federation of Trade Unions) on equal basis with the Jewish workers, and why are they discriminated against in employment and wages? Or why are there land confiscation laws from which only Arabs, and a large number of them, have suffered?"

He certainly was intending to go on asking *why*, but I had to stop him for I could hardly deny any of the accusations he made. "But, my friend," I reminded him, "do you not think that for security reasons the government has to take precautions? Do you not also agree that economic and social progress, or change I should say, do not come overnight?" He agreed, but he also remembered that it had been ten years since the establishment of the State and that these Arabs had not proved to be disloyal to the State of Israel. But that was not all he had to say, because I could see from his pause that something very important was on his mind.

"You know," he said, "these Israeli Arabs who are more than 10 percent of the population can create a real headache for the State of Israel! Just recall how much trouble the Jews caused in Palestine during the British Mandate, when they were a small minority. Think also of the Turkish and French minorities in Cyprus and Algeria, respectively, and you will be able to imagine the role the Israeli Arabs can play in Israel. Are not the Turkish Cypriots and the Algerian French already contemplating partition so as to achieve autonomy, and if so, why cannot the Israeli Arabs do the same? In fact, their attempts would have more moral strength since most of them live on the territory that lies outside the borders allocated for the State of Israel by the United Nations."

Although I maintained silence during most of the latter discussion, except for a question or a comment here and there, I could not be uninterested in his argument, particularly since all the Arabic literature I have received from Israel indicates that conditions of the Arabs there have not only failed to improve since my departure, but that they have considerably deteriorated. It also is interesting to note that some Arabic periodicals published in Israel, which were too complacent in the early years of statehood, have become very daring in handling these problems, especially those issued on the occasion of the tenth anniversary of the State of Israel. If anything, the change in the tone only supports my companion's theory that the patience of the Israeli Arabs may also reach an end and that it would be unwise for the State of Israel to ignore these facts or to deal with them inhumanly. On the contrary, he insisted that it might prove fruitful if the Government of Israel improved the conditions of these Arabs and tried to utilize their influence in promoting mutual understanding with Arab refugees and Arab countries. Furthermore, it would afford an opportunity for the State of Israel, in dealing with its Arab citizens, to show a sign of good will and demonstrate the ability of Jews and Arabs to live together peacefully and as good neighbors.

Three months have passed and still my companion's question rings in my mind: *What have you Israelis done to promote peace with the Arabs!*

The conditions have changed dramatically since I wrote those recollections, but the obstacles to peace have remained the same. Israel has enlarged the area under occupation and the Arab community within its de facto borders. The Arab countries have suffered another defeat and thus developed more hate toward their opponents. The Palestinians have become a little more organized, active, and destructive against Israel and some Arab states. All parties are still as unrealistic in approaching peace and as dishonest about their peace gestures as they were then. The Arabs are still demanding the impossible; Israel is still arrogantly doing nothing tangible to promote a peace agreement; and the foreign powers are still exploiting the conflict for their own interests. Even the United Nations is still contradictory in passing resolutions with full knowledge that they will not be implemented. Hence peace efforts have been doomed or futile.

Peacemaking depends on good will and recognition of one's situation. A combination of the two would ensure progress toward peace. Recognition of the situation means that each party knows what prospects are available and would make the best out of these prospects. However, good will is also essential since peace-making requires some readiness to make sacrifices, to cooperate with the other party, and to abide by any agreements made. The failure of peace efforts in the Middle East suggests that good intentions have been lacking or at least have not been strong enough to bring about peace.

Strictly speaking, peacemaking in the Middle East dates back to 1948 only. Prior to that date there was no Israeli state and presumably the Arabs and the Jews were not in a state of war. Both were involved in guerrilla warfare against the British, but Britain was withdrawing and peacemaking was not meaningful. Britain did try to create some understanding with both parties by means of the White Paper, issued in 1939 to end the Arab rebellion. The White Paper was a sort of pacifier and not a successful one at that; it promised things that could not be delivered, such as the limitation of Jewish immigration and a kind of reconciliation between the interests of Arabs and Jews. Yet once the holocaust against the Jews in Europe became known, Britain was unable and unwilling to limit immigration. Once immigration, legal or illegal, had been expanded, the conflict of interests became imminent. Other than these efforts, peacemaking had to wait until after World War II, at which time a United Nations commission began the search for a solution. That was the beginning of the era of futile peacemaking and abortive attempts to end the immoral war. The year 1947 marked the beginning of the state of war. Britain decided to end the Mandate, the United Nations gave legitimacy to an Israeli state, and the Jewish and Zionist leaders were ready to announce the birth of the state. The Arab armies invaded the borders of Palestine in order to prevent the creation of Israel, or at least pretended to do so. War was declared and has continued ever since, although all parties pretend to be anxious to promote peace. If so, why is there no peace? At the cost of extreme oversimplification, it may be said that neither party has been serious enough about peace to take the initiative or accept the responsibilities entailed by peace. Let us look at these efforts and the reasons that they failed.

II

The Israeli efforts for peace have been vague, uncoordinated, and on the whole, arrogant and uncompromising. It is true that Israel has reasons to be worried and untrusting, given the attitude of the Arabs and the provocations uttered by their leaders. Some observers have suggested that Israel is actually anxious to maintain a state of suspense and insecurity in order to recruit the necessary support from the outside and to complete the integration of incoming Jews with the emerging Israeli society. I would like to suggest that Israel has been under no real pressure to bring about peace. Its economic and political security have been guaranteed by the western powers and the Jewish communities all over the world. Furthermore, the war atmosphere has brought gains and has put Israel in such a strong position that any peace arrangement it might conclude is bound to entail some territorial losses or reduction in the gains realized so far. Therefore, Israeli proposals for peace have not been serious invitations to pursue peace. A few examples will illustrate.

In 1953, Foreign Minister Moshe Sharett, who was considered a moderate, declared that Israel had only one condition for peace: "It is that we should be accepted and accepted *as we are*, with our territory, population, and unrestricted sovereignty. We seek no encroachment on the integrity or sovereignty of our neighbors, and are at a loss to understand how they can legitimately make such encroachments on us the condition of a settlement"[7] Sharett was too intelligent to accept the logic of his own argument. He knew very well that Israel had already done its encroaching and would be happy to be accepted as such. By choosing the point of departure for peace, Israel had an advantage and could pretend to be an innocent, peace-loving nation. That same attitude was reiterated by Aba Eban in 1965 when he rejected as artificial the idea that a price must be paid for peace, that peace is something to be bought. "If Arab minds were able to make peace with Israel at all, they would be able to make . . . peace

---

[7]Samuel Merlin, *The Search for Peace in the Middle East* (South Brunswick, New York: Thomas Yoseloff, 1968), p. 187.

with Israel as it is: not with Israel as it was not and is not and will not be."[8] As a diplomat, Aba Eban is known for his play with words, but he also knows that such expressions, even if they are meant only for propaganda and public consumption, are bound to poison the air for any peacemaking efforts.

These may seem to be isolated statements and not at all representative of Israel's attitude, but even the more articulate and detailed statements contain the same ambiguity and arrogance. Under the mounting pressure to respond to the initiative of President Bourguiba of Tunisia, Prime Minister Eshkol outlined a plan in the Knesset in May 1965 in which he stated, among other things:

"Peace will be established on the basis of Israel as it is . . ."; minor boundary changes may be made but that is all; the Arabs will refrain from aggression; open transport and communications will be promoted between Israel and her neighbors; trade will be instituted; arid areas will be cultivated; negotiation will lead to restraint in the arms race; resources freed through disarmament and contributions by Israel will be used to settle the refugees in Arab countries.[9] Eshkol and most other Israelis knew that that was not a plan for peace; it just pointed out what the benefits of a peace with Israel "as it is" would be. Needless to say, no other party was convinced of the geniuneness of the Israeli response to Bourguiba.

In 1968, Aba Eban, as foreign minister, addressed the United Nations General Assembly and presented "the nine principles by which peace can be achieved": The cease-fire must be followed by a permanent well-defined peace; within the framework of peace secure boundaries will be established; security agreements will be concluded in addition to secure boundaries; freedom of movement across boundaries

[8] *Ibid.*, p. 187.
[9] *Ibid.*, p. 212–213.

will be promoted; the international waterways will be open for all navigation; the refugee problem will be treated by a conference that would chart a five-year plan and by a joint integration and rehabilitation commission; as an Israeli initiative the unification of families will be accelerated; Christian and Moslem holy places in Jerusalem would be "under the responsibility of those who hold them in reverence"; mutual recognition of national sovereignty would be declared; and regional cooperation would be sought.[10] As such, this is a comprehensive, vague, one-sided, and unrealistic plan. It lumps all issues together; it commits Israel to nothing; it legitimizes the occupation of territory taken in the 1967 war. Even the concept of "Israel as it is" is given a new meaning —it is made dynamic so as to leave room for Israeli expansion by war or other means. Did Aba Eban expect any results from his initiative, or was this another of his eloquent exercises in rhetoric and big talk?

These same principles have been repeated again and again. In May 1969, Prime Minister Golda Meir outlined the position of Israel in the Knesset: Peace must be a direct agreement between Israel and her neighbors; no imposition from the outside would be tolerated; peace treaties would define "agreed, secure, and recognized boundaries"; peace treaties "must annul claims of belligerency, blockade, boycotts, interference with free navigation," and all sabotage activities. Such a peace treaty would preclude any regional pacts that may be concluded against any state in the region.[11] Here again Israel outlines what a peace treaty should do, but not how it could be reached or what concessions Israel will

[10]U.S. Congress, Committee on Foreign Relations, *A Select Chronology and Background Documents Relating to the Middle East*, Washington, 1969, pp. 270–273.

[11]Harry B. Ellis, *The Dilemma of Israel* (Washington D.C.: American Enterprise Institute, October 1970), pp. 38–39.

make to achieve it. In fact, such a plan simply required the Arabs to recognize Israel and negotiate, but Israel commits itself to nothing. Recognition of Israel is the least Israel can expect, but to make this a condition and to leave everything else vague and uncommitted renders the Israeli position untenable. Obviously Israel is in a position of strength at the present time and apparently feels that no concessions are necessary; probably peace itself is not necessary either!

The most recent initiative for peace, by the United States and the United Nations, has brought Israel a little closer to reality. A ceasefire on the Suez Canal and the new undertaking by Gunnar Jarring have been reluctantly agreed to by Israel. Now we are told that Israel has indeed made many concessions: "It accepted the procedure of indirect negotiations; it agreed to a limited ceasefire and concluded an agreement with Egypt on this and on a military standstill; it agreed to New York as the site of the talks, dropping its original request that the talks be held at a venue closer to the Middle East; and it agreed not to make an issue out of the Arab refusal to delegate their foreign ministers to the talks as Jarring had requested. Indeed, it may be said in retrospect that no other party did so much and risked as much in order to assure the start of the Jarring talks as did Israel in August 1970."[12] How significant are these concessions? Not a single count relates to substance; all are matters of procedure and bargaining tactics. And these were made, most probably, after the United States had assured Israel of security and arms and actually followed it later with $500 million in arms aid. So far we have no Israeli plan for peace and no commitments on substance. The Israelis want peace at no price; they want it on their own conditions; they want it but not badly

---

[12]Embassy of Israel, "The Jarring Talks: Israel's Third Try," *Policy Background*, January 1971.

enough to commit themselves in advance to any concession, despite the tension under which the people in Israel live. (Some observers regard that tension as a normal state of affairs in Israel.)[13] Indeed, Israel continues to boast of its military strength, to build up its weapon arsenal, and to participate in an immoral war for which it is as much responsible as any other party.

III

Lest the reader be easily misled by my condemnation of Israel's failure to help in peacemaking, let me hasten to add that the Arabs have not been any more realistic, honest, or anxious to promote peace. The Arabs have presented many plans for peace, but they are virtually monolithic in content. They have made many errors which have cost them dearly. While trying to correct these errors they commit new ones which complicate the situation even further. Some of these errors are their inability to face reality, their unwillingness to compromise, and their insistence on all or nothing solutions (hence they end up with nothing), and their lack of compassion both toward their own people and toward the Jews who may be honestly seeking a home and a refuge. Their peace plans on the whole reflect their errors.

The Arabs often have emphasized what they will not do rather than what they will do: They will not negotiate with Israel directly; they will not recognize Israel as a state; they will not settle the Arab refugees. However, they have armed themselves with resolutions of the United Nations and have insisted on their implementation regardless of whether these

[13]Amnon Rubenstein, "Israel asks, 'Ma ihieh hassof?' What will be the end?," *New York Times Magazine*, May 31, 1970, pp. 5ff.

resolutions make sense as practical solutions. Furthermore, the demands of the Arabs have changed little over time, although the conditions have changed. They still dream of a situation which they rejected in 1947, even though they are certain that that situation cannot be re-created peacefully, or even unpeacefully. As conditions were changed by the 1956 and 1967 wars, emphasis has shifted to short-run adjustments, such as withdrawal from the occupied territories, but no modification of the earlier position has accompanied that shift, at least not openly. Here a great contradiction seems to prevail: The Arab countries now emphasize the short-run objectives of withdrawal, while the long-run objectives are upheld mainly by the Palestinian Arabs. The two groups of Arabs do not see eye-to-eye on these matters; yet the Arab governments have not had the courage to declare the change in their attitude or to face reality and make the best out of the situation. Even when they have been in direct and bloody conflict with the Palestinians, they have not had the courage to take a stand against the war that the Palestinians fight with little hope of winning—at least not in the foreseeable future. The peace proposals of the Arabs have been consistent with these contradictory and divided attitudes, and hence they have been doomed to fail. Let us look at some of these proposals in some detail.

There have been at least four different Arab approaches to peace, though not always admitted as such. For convenience, these approaches may be classified as: the undoing of history; the unified state; the half-way approach; and the gradualist vague approach.

1. The first approach, which is held by some official and many unofficial spokesmen, suggests the undoing of history, the return to the prestate era, the return of both Arabs and Jews to where they came from, and the creation of a Palestinian state in the territory previously held by British Man-

date. This approach cannot be taken seriously in the context of peacemaking because no party that has any relevance to the conflict would agree to it. The fact that Arab leaders make such a suggestion can mean only one of two things: either that they use it as a delaying tactic or that they have lost the right perspective and hence their proposal is symptomatic of an imbalance in their ability to comprehend the situation. They have invoked what they call justice and in its name have proposed the movement of about 75 percent of the population of Israel and of most of the former Palestinians from their present residences. They propose that the Jews who have worked for almost a century to reach the stage they are in now should forget all their achievements, sufferings, dislocations, and hopes and wipe the statehood of Israel from existence. This proposal can best be evaluated by ignoring it. It has neither logic nor realism.

2. The Palestinian Arabs have been consistent in rejecting the partition of Palestine and the creation of two separate states, Arab and Jewish, although for about 15 years prior to 1965 they entertained the idea of a return to the United Nations Partition Plan of 1947. During that period they were acquiescent to the demands of the Arab states. The upsurge of various organizations to liberate Palestine has brought with it independent proposals for peace which are revivals of the early attitude against partition. The most prominent of these is the proposal of Fatah for a unified state. Put simply this proposal advocates that Palestine be unified as it was under the Mandate; that Arabs and Jews form a state on secular grounds; and that all ethnic, religious, and social groups live together in a democratic state. This proposal has been espoused by intellectuals, commandoes, and many others who are more pro-Arab and less pro-Israel. Proponents of this plan regard it as capable of meeting what they consider a good test for a workable solution. The Palestinian peace

plan gives "advantage to Arab and Jew alike." It is fair to the Jews; it is a long-term solution; and it is realistic in that it takes into consideration the expected changes in the situation. These changes include the awakening of the Palestinian Arabs and pressures to regulate the expansionism of Israel. Most important, it recognizes that the Palestinians have no way to go but to advance socially, economically, and technologically, in which case they would be a threat to the existence of their opponents. Given these expectations, the Palestinian plan is considered realistic.

While the significance of this plan to Israel, as a party to the conflict, or to the external powers may be minimal, it is quite influential with respect to the Palestinians. It is sufficient to draw support and sustain opposition to peaceful solutions and may in the long-run close the minds of the Palestinians to any other solution that may be practical and meaningful. For this reason, I should like to analyze this approach in detail and show its faults and uselessness as an effort toward peace. This proposal, in my estimation, is unrealistic and definitely unacceptable to all those who support an independent Israel. It is also very harmful to the Arabs in both the short and the long run and therefore should be reconsidered and even rejected by the Palestinians themselves.

I think that the Arabs who have espoused this plan have done so with full awareness of its impracticality. They have adopted it because it serves the political objectives of recruiting support abroad as a plan based on democracy, harmony, and justice. Hence, all those who oppose it would be accused of being opposed to these values. At the same time, even if the plan were to be adopted, the Arabs are not honest about their intentions and why they want it. What they propose is a society in which the Arabs would be a majority and thus would eventually control the country and reduce Jewish influence to insignificance. Unfortunately, many Arabs believe in the strategic significance of this plan when, in fact, it is harmful and impractical. The plan is unrealistic because it expects the Zionists, Jewish, and Israeli leaders to abolish the Jewishness of the State of Israel, to give up the idea of a national home as they understand it, and to help to create a situation in which they may become a minority. This is preposterous to propose, and it is an insult to Arab intellect to even present such a plan with any degree of seriousness.

Nevertheless, let us assume for the moment that such a plan can be implemented. Will it work? I do not think so. The Arabs and the Jews are both very nationalistic; both have suffered and are anxious to have rehabilitation and restoration of self-respect; however, they are of unequal education and technical skill, business aggressiveness, and entrepreneurship. These inequalities are bound to continue for many years, even though they may be diminishing. The result of a unified society will be a division between a majority and a minority, in terms of numbers, and between a strong group and a weak group, in terms of qualifications. The numbers usually will be superseded by the qualifications, and accordingly, a certain kind of imperialism is bound to develop. The strong minority will dominate the weak majority; the Jews will dominate and the Arabs will be in a position either to submit or to rise and seek revenge. This is far from a democratic, unified state, as suggested by the Palestinians who are preaching their new love of democracy.

The defects of this plan can be easily demonstrated by observing the falsely glorified harmony between Arabs and Jews in Israel. Actually there is no harmony, trust, or meaningful democracy as far as the Arabs are concerned. I have lived through those conditions and have observed them carefully. I have found no reason to change my views on these relations. I am still convinced that the Arabs and Jews cannot live in harmony and equality in the same state unless they are

willing and able to forget Arab nationalism and Jewish Zionism, which neither can be expected to do. I have always
raised questions as to "what lies ahead for those Arabs in
Israel who form an island within an island"; the answer has
not been a happy one, but it is as real as I can make it. Let
me reproduce excerpts of my observations, written in 1966,
for clarity:[14]

The Arabs of Israel are not a community in the sociological sense.
They are not a nation, nor part of a nation. They are neither here
nor there in the conflict between Israel and her Arab neighbors.
They are Arabs but not one with the Arab states; they live in Israel
but do not form an integral part of it.

They just live, in a state of disorganization, distrust, and despair.
The best description I have for their condition is that they suffer
from a high degree of demoralization which, unless checked soon,
may lead into a hopeless situation. This is particularly true of the
younger generation who have known no other happier times.

As a visitor to Arab villages and towns, I was struck by the amount
of new construction. New houses have been and are being built
everywhere, and the people made it their business to draw my
attention to and comment on their expansion and prosperity. Some
villages have doubled their size in these ten years. They assured me
that everybody was working, except for some middle-aged people
who had chosen to retire prematurely because their children were
working and they could afford it. The people worked in construction, in workshops and factories, in Jewish farms, and some in white-
collar jobs. Many were school teachers earning a "lot" of money; at
least so it appeared to them since many families still pooled the
earnings of all the members to finance any project they undertook.

These symptoms of prosperity were brought into focus by the
officials I met, whether Arabs or Jews, from the chauffeur who drove
me around to the highest official I came in contact with. The Arab
officials, however, often changed their attitude when they hap-
pened to see me alone or if they knew me well. The officials pointed
out the new construction, the few schools that had been built, the

---

[14]Elias H. Tuma, "The Arabs in Israel: An Impasse," *New Outlook*, March–
April, 1966, pp. 39–46.

number of students going to universities, the tractors that had replaced the wooden plough, and the full employment among the Arabs. They admitted that there might be some exceptions, but these exceptions or failures usually were the result of internal disunity among the Arabs, lack of cooperation and leadership, or simply due to a time lag and would certainly be corrected in time. The government, they told me, was doing all it could to improve the situation, and the rest was up to the people themselves. However, no one said anything about the decline of farming, the low quality of education, the frustration and grievances of the Arabs, or the dim prospects that face the young Arabs in the country.

Reasons for distrust

Had I not been especially curious, I might have left these people admiring their achievements and appreciating the prosperity they have been enjoying within the State. Soon, however, it became apparent that all was not well and that underneath that thin layer of prosperity many deep-seated fears and insecurities lay dormant. Even without directing questions I heard sad stories repeated again and again, with such a tone of monotony that it was hardly possible to doubt the truth of their complaints. For example, every person who builds a house in the village anticipates going to court and paying a fine for building without a license. The fine may go up to IL 1,000, or a three-months salary of a new school teacher, and may be repeated every six months until a license has been secured. Yet he builds without a license because licenses are not issued until a zoning map has been approved by the Ministry of the Interior. Such maps are not being approved, according to some, because the government is receiving a sizable revenue from the fines. Or the proposed maps are not approved because they include certain locations in the village land which the government insists on reserving for Jewish settlement, and until then, that land must remain free of construction. The people are convinced that the government had bad intentions toward their land and was doing all it could to expropriate them by what might seem like legal procedures.

To prove their point, many Arabs I talked with reminded me of how the government expropriated land from the villages of Bi'na and Deir al Asad to build the town of Carmiel in Western Galilee. The expropriation proceeded first and attempts for settlement of the claims followed later, on conditions unacceptable to the owners. For example, the owners who were expropriated were offered compensation at a rate of about IL 250 per dunam (one quarter of an acre) though the market price of the same was about IL 5,000. The terms of compensation were "take it or leave it." Another way of expropriation used was the arbitrary enforcement of the law on wasteland. According to the law, an unimproved piece of land is subject to expropriation, yet if the owner agreed to surrender a given lot in a different locality in its stead, he was allowed to keep it regardless of how unimproved it was.

Though I listened attentively to these charges, now it seems unimportant whether the charges are true or not. It is more important that they are so common and that mistrust of the intentions of the government toward Arab land pervades all ranks. It is equally significant that the government has done little to disprove the charges or to alleviate the grievances. The law courts continue to impose fines, and Jewish settlements continue to rise on Arab land. If the above methods of expropriation do not suffice, the land designated for expropriation is marked as a military zone to which no entry permits are issued and thus the land is de facto lost. In fairness to the government, many people told me that land is sometimes offered in exchange for these appropriated territories. However, most expropriated owners find the terms of exchange unacceptable. If someone happens to approve of the principle of exchange, usually he is requested to surrender his title deed retroactively as of 1946 or 1947, but in return he is given the new land *only to hold by agreement*. The expropriated owner refuses, particularly when the land he is offered is part of the "abandoned" property of a former Palestinian Arab who is a refugee. In other words, the exchange implies surrendering a title deed without acquiring one in its place, which he refuses to accept.

The grievances I heard against the land policy had no end, but certainly these were not the only grievances. The Israeli Arabs felt that the government was pursuing policies that would ultimately lead to their destruction as farmers. They claimed that the government guaranteed different prices for Arab and Jewish tobacco growers, and that those guaranteed for Arab farmers hardly covered the production costs. And in fact, one cannot fail to observe that Ar have given up farming. Some have become dependent on their wage-working children, while others confess that farming has ceased to be profitable. As a result there has been a rapid drift of Arabs into wage-labor in Jewish enterprises. Very few are in the professions and still less in trade and commerce, except for the retailers who cater to Arab clientele in Arab localities. The Arabs believe that they are recruited to do the "dirty" work or because they accept lower wages by accepting lower grading than their Jewish counterparts.

AFRAID TO TALK

I heard these complaints everywhere and from people from all walks of life, but primarily from the self-employed or from wage-workers. Teachers, social workers, and white-collar employees refrained from talking unless I managed to see each one separately. Then it appeared that they were in full sympathy with these charges, but they were afraid to talk, lest someone hear them and report what they say to the military governor. They would trust no one since everyone was a potential informer. In every village, they said, there were at least a hundred informers, among whom were simple workers, teachers, spiritual leaders, or political representatives. These informers were accredited with the power to transfer teachers and employees, to dismiss them, or to appoint new ones. Therefore, those who held salaried jobs thought it wiser to be silent if they wanted to keep their jobs.

The views expressed by my Jewish friends, as well as by officials, were restrained. They indicated the progress attained and suggested that it was up to the Arabs to decide whether they can be happy or not. As one highranking official put it, "This is the way things are. We are in a democracy, and the minority must obey the majority. They are living better than do the Arabs under Nasser. If they do not like us, let them get out." Another person closely associated with land settlement put it differently, "We have no other alternative; even if we wanted the Arabs out of the country, the international community would not permit it. Therefore, we'll just ʾave to try to live together peacefully." In essence, the official ʾy is simply this: "If the Arabs want to stay, why not? Let them

stay so long as they do not interfere with our long-term plans and
as long as they behave themselves. We need laborers, and they
provide them. As long as they are disorganized, and the military
government sees to that, they are harmless."

WHAT ABOUT THE FUTURE?

The Arabs themselves were more passive about their future.
Their common response was, "We do not know." Those who had
thought about the question admitted that they had no hope for a
future. They could do nothing, so they just live. The younger generation seemed fatalistic, without ambition or thought of the future.
The ones who were outspoken were anxious to leave the country,
but they did not know how or where to go.

This is the impasse. The talk about the future unveils the dilemma
of both the Arabs and the Jews in Israel. The Arabs are Israelis, but
less so than the Jews. They are free and equal, but less so than the
Jews. They are tolerated but not trusted. They listen to the Voice
of the Arabs from Cairo, but they owe loyalty to Israel. They have
given little reason to create mistrust and yet they are deeply mis-
trusted. A few cases of border crossing or espionage are common in
all countries, but in Israel such incidents assume extra significance
because of the enmity with the surrounding Arab neighbors. While
the State may be justified in guarding its security, the Arabs of the
country pay a price for what they have not committed. Any suspi-
cion of deviation from the path drawn for them by the authorities
is subject to misinterpretation and may be detrimental. Any period
of economic or political crisis in Israel is bound to increase the
probabilities of misinterpretation, discrimination, and persecution.
When unemployment prevailed in the mid-fifties, Jewish workers
were given emergency relief work which included the responsibility to chase unorganized and Arab labor from industrial and commercial Jewish outfits. More recently, when Syria condemned an
Israeli Jew on a charge of espionage, the Jews of Acre started attack-
ing Arabs wherever they found them. A few days after I left the
country in mid-August, an automobile accident involving Arabs and
Jews was followed by a Jewish riot which resulted in the injury of
twelve Arabs in the town of Ramlah. Is there any reason to believe

that similar incidents will not occur every time something antago-
nizes the Jewish communities in Israel? In fact, even if a peace
treaty were concluded with the Arab states, is there any assurance
that any disturbance to the peace or any economic crisis in the
country will not mean trouble to the Israeli Arabs from their fellow
citizens? The very unhappy consequences that might happen in the
more serious case of a military clash with the Arab states can only
be surmised.

Before looking for a solution I should like to dispel a widely held
conviction that the size of the Arab minority in Israel will be enlarged when the Arab refugees return from across the borders, and
therefore their status will improve. The same belief holds that with
the return of the refugees, the borders of the state will be modified
in accordance with the 1947 Partition Plan, and thus most of the
Arabs will be relocated automatically outside Israel and their problem will vanish. Both beliefs are questionable for several reasons.
First, it is reasonable to suggest that the refugee problem should be
separated from that of the borders, the one being primarily a humane problem, the other political. Second, should the refugees
return and live within Israel, they will still be a minority. The
difficulties faced by the present Israeli Arab will simply be common
to a large minority. The lag between the Arabs, particularly the
potential returnees, and the Jews in the economic and social conditions and institutions will almost by necessity render the Arabs
economically and politically subordinate to and dependent on the
Jewish majority, regardless of the good intentions that may prevail.
Third, a more realistic approach to the refugee question would
suggest that there is no sound basis for expecting the refugees to
return, nor is it practical or beneficial for them to do so, given the
present social and economic structure of the country. And politically, it seems highly improbable that they will return. Therefore,
it is of the utmost importance for the present Arab minority to look
for alternative outlets from the dilemma.

While assurances cannot be given that the recurrence of unhappy
incidents can be prevented, or that a change of policy to improve
the social and political conditions of the Arabs fundamentally is
forthcoming, the present policy of wait and see may have any of the
following results:

1) A further intensification of the current trend. The Arabs will
simply "grin and bear it." They will experience the destruction of

their cultural heritage, continue to suffer imaginary or real discrimination, lose their identity, and survive as strangers and suspects in
their own land. Their second-class citizen status, which was a political fabrication in the early years of the State, will be perpetuated
by acquiring an economic basis in the form of high dependence on
wage-labor, the decline of Arab agriculture, and the small stake
they have in the professions. That will be the consummation of what
has already been started.

2) Another possible result of this policy of do-nothing may be
the complete assimilation of the Arabs into the Jewish community.
Should that happen, the Arabs will vanish as a group but save themselves as individuals by assuming the identity of the majority and
giving up their present Arab identity. However, complete assimilation is highly improbable even though a certain degree of assimila-
tin has already taken place. Now most young Arabs speak Hebrew
fluently. Many read Hebrew newspapers. Some have become so
anxious to assimilate that they mix every sentence of Arabic they
use with a word or two of Hebrew, even when they are talking
among themselves. They have adjusted to Saturday as the weekly
holiday, and some date Jewish girls. But that is the end of their
assimilation: they do not intermarry; they use Arabic as the language of instruction and attend separate schools; they have their
own religion; and they maintain a certain affinity towards the Arabs
across the borders, whether they are refugees and relatives or Arabs
at large. Furthermore, assimilation is hindered by official policies
that still handle Arab affairs through separate government depart-
ments. Therefore, while assimilation might be desirable, it is highly
improbable.

3) But out of the ashes may come fire, and out of this greatly
demoralized Arab group new leaders may arise who will manage to
reorganize them and save them from cultural annihilation. Should
such leadership succeed in establishing itself, it is very likely that
they would demand full rights through internal autonomy. Experience shows that organized movements for internal autonomy have
usually erupted into violence, bloodshed, and an international crisis.

If this is the situation when the Jews are a majority and the
Arabs a minority, why should we expect that the relationship
would be better if the Arabs were the majority and the Jews

the minority? The Palestinian solution has no documentation to show that it can work, even if the parties concerned were interested in trying. Religious conflict in Ireland, national division in India and Pakistan, ethnic and religious separatism in Cyprus, and the previous history of the Jews suggest the opposite of that which the Palestinian solution envisages. Given the accumulated hatred over more than two decades, one would expect that the conditions would be worse if the Arabs were suddenly to become the majority and the Jews a minority in Palestine. It seems that this solution is not realistic because the Jews are not likely to take it seriously and because it cannot work as long as Arab or Jewish nationalism is as strong as it is at present. A small minority is bound to lose its national identity; a large minority is bound to resist, resulting in bloodshed and imminent failure.

This solution is bound to meet with resistance from certain Arab states. More specifically, it is doubtful whether King Hussein of Jordan would cede that part of Palestine, which has been annexed, to join with Israel as a unified state. The bloody conflict between the Palestinians and the Jordanian army testifies to the potential conflict should the Palestinians have their way. Therefore, the solution proposed by the Palestinians has been doomed and can hardly be used to promote peace.

(3). The "half-way" solution has been the usual approach by Egypt, Jordan, and a majority of the other Arab states. The various proposals, if they may be called that, made by the Arabs were half-way in the sense that they usually covered that which would benefit only the Arabs and did not consider the problem from the other side as well. These proposals always stopped short of agreeing to recognize Israel, of talking directly with the Israelis, and of anticipating the signing of a peace agreement. When pressed on these points, the Arabs either evaded the question or rejected the idea of reaching that far. Furthermore, Arab proposals have more frequently been either reiterations of United Nations resolutions or responses to questions and initiatives of others. We shall deal with the United Nations resolutions separately. Here we will evaluate Arab responses and those proposals that can be identified. Between 1948 and 1967 there were few proposals other than demands for implementation of the United Nations resolutions. However, after the 1967 war and the occupation of vast areas by Israel, the Arab states began to speak of plans for settlement of the conflict. In an interview in 1968, President Nasser outlined his views of a settlement by focusing on two points: the evacuation of all the occupied territories and the repatriation of the refugees. Once Israel had met these demands, Nassar promised "a peaceful settlement in spite of what took place during the last 20 or more years."[15] It is interesting, however, that Nasser specified the borders of June 1, 1967 as the basis of settlement, not those proposed by the United Nations before the 1948 war. He knew, of course, that Israel had already declared its intentions to retain parts of the newly occupied areas. When questioned about the security of Israel and its withdrawal from the territories occupied in 1967, he proposed "(1) a declaration of nonbeligerance; (2) the right of each country to live in peace; (3) the territorial integrity of all countries in the Middle East, including Israel, in recognized and secure borders; (4) freedom of navigation on international waterways; (5) a just solution to the Palestinian refugee problem."[16] With minor changes in wording, a similar proposal was made by King Hussein in a speech at the National Press Club in Washington in April 1969, to which Nasser was said to have agreed.

[15] *New York Times*, March 2, 1969, p. 28.
[16] U.S. Congress, Senate, Foreign Relations Committee, *A Select Chronology and Background Documents*, 1969, pp. 276–77.

Strangely enough, these plans have much in common with those outlined by Aba Eban and by Golda Meir in 1968 and 1969, respectively, but there has been no progress toward peace. What prevented these "willing" nations from reaching an agreement? Probably the only clear point is that neither side had honest and good intentions; both parties were full of mutual distrust and unwillingness to compromise. When they found themselves in agreement on substance, they managed to disagree on procedure and form. For example, neither Nasser nor Hussein would agree to the direct negotiations which Israel had stipulated. Neither would declare readiness to sign a peace treaty; they simply asserted that each country would have the right to live in peace. Although they spoke of fair and just settlement of the refugee problem, they usually meant the right of the Palestinians to repatriation, which Israel already had ruled out. It would be a great oversimplification to think that the Arabs expected peace to result from their proposals.

This pattern of proposals and counterproposals by the Arab states and Israel is being repeated at the present time as a response to the United States initiative for peace. Having agreed to a ceasefire on the Suez Canal, Israel, and Egypt again are making the same demands of each other, with little hope that the other party will accept. Egypt, for example, in January 1971, publicized a new peace proposal which includes: (1) withdrawal of Israel behind the June 5, 1967 borders; (2) a declaration by Israel repudiating "the policy of territorial expansion" with the idea of limiting immigration into Israel; (3) a just settlement of the refugee problem based on "respect of the rights of the Palestinian people"; (4) termination of all belligerency and a guarantee of freedom of navigation; (5) respect of sovereignty and territorial integrity of all states in the region; (6) guarantee of the peace, security, and political independence of all nations, under supervision of the United Nations Security Council.[17] At face value this proposal seems comprehensive and accomodating until it becomes known that no declaration of intent to sign a peace treaty with Israel is provided. Nor is the question of Palestinian repatriation rights fully defined, and there is no indication of the firmness of the demand to withdraw beyond the June 5 boundaries. Yet Israel seems unwilling to compromise on these issues. Furthermore, the Arab proposal implies a contradiction: on one hand, it declares respect for national sovereignty, and on the other, it expects a certain limitation of Jewish immigration to Israel. Aba Eban expressed it correctly when he said that Israel does not ask Egypt to restrict its birth rate; why should Egypt interfere with Jewish immigration into Israel? The main point is that a proposal such as this is bound to fail. To regard the proposal as only a beginning of the bargaining process may be worthwhile if the cost of waiting is quite low or nonexistent. At present, the cost of delaying is rather high and bargaining implies additional suffering by large groups of people. Israel has already rejected these proposals. Though many diplomats and official spokesmen continue to make optimistic declarations, there is no evidence that optimism is warranted. I can find little that is encouraging in these proposals.

(4). The "gradualist approach" is primarily what President Bourguiba of Tunisia advocated in regard to the Arab-Israeli conflict. Bourguiba's approach was based on several premises: that the conflict is mainly a Palestinian affair; that the conflict is the result of a chain of errors by Arab leaders; that it is becoming more complicated because Arab leaders have diffused the issue of Palestine with their internal politics and with inter-Arab affairs in general; that an all-or-nothing ap-

---

[17] *Sacramento Bee*, January 21, 1971, p. 18.

proach is not a wise approach; and that the war cannot be won although battles may be won. Bourguiba was proposing a more political and less violent approach. He thought that a compromise that at least temporarily accepts a partial settlement would be better than no settlement.

Bourguiba was concerned more with procedure than with substance, which he regarded as a Palestinian concern. He proposed indirectly that negotiations with Israel should be conducted. Beyond that Bourguiba proposed no known plans for peace. Unfortunately neither his supporters nor Israel were ready to build on what he had started. Israel considered his proposals vague, noncommital, and possibly dishonest. His proposal was actually doomed to the extent that it did not spell out matters of substance and had opposition of the parties most involved in the conflict. The proposal met its fate in due course.

IV

Probably the greatest peacemaking effort has been undertaken by the United Nations. It is depressing to find so little success as a result of these efforts. The problem lies to a large extent in the structure of the United Nations and the lack of sufficient commitment by its membership to the concept of the United Nations. The United Nations is a collection of individual member countries, each with its own national interests and biases. Its members play various roles simultaneously. These roles often conflict with each other; the members compromise on certain objectives for the sake of others. The structure of the United Nations as a peacemaking organization is weakened by two major factors: the differential distribution of real power, especially as represented by the veto power which is enjoyed by the five permanent members of the Security Council, and the organization's lack of power to implement its resolutions. Its effectiveness depends mainly on the moral commitment of its members and their willingness to abide by the resolutions of the agency at large.

The United Nations can, in fact, be held responsible for the failure of peacemaking and for continuation of the conflict, not only because of what it has done but also because of what it has failed to do. On one hand, the United Nations has legitimized the existence of Israel but has been unable to influence the behavior of Israel or its expansion. It passed a Partition Plan for Palestine, but this was ignored. It voted for upholding the rights of the Palestinians but has been unable to implement policies that guarantee these rights. It has passed a resolution demanding withdrawal of Israel from the territories occupied in 1967 but has been unable to enforce that resolution. Its resolutions upholding the right of Israel to use the international waterways have not been enforced. The resolutions regarding the Holy Places have also been ignored, and the United Nations has been unable to do anything about it.

The fact that the United Nations has not been able to do much about these questions is not what constitutes the failure. It is its inflexibility which constitutes failure. The United Nations has not seen fit to modify its stand on the partition of Palestine; it has failed to modify its stand on the repatriation of the Arab refugees and the political status of the Holy Places. The conditions surrounding these issues have changed so radically that the original resolutions have become virtually irrelevant. Yet, these same resolutions remain on the books and constitute what the Arabs regard as the framework for just solutions to the conflict. As long as the United Nations continues to reiterate these resolutions, the Arabs will continue to argue that justice is on their side although they know that these resolutions are no longer relevant or applicable. Israel also knows that those resolutions are no longer relevant and that the United Nations has no means for or interest in enforcing these resolutions, and therefore Israel has no reason to submit to them. The conflict persists; the United Nations continues to debate and to pass resolutions which are interpreted by each party according to its own interests, and each party invokes the United Nations resolutions to defend its moral position. The peace plans sponsored by the United Nations might be morally sound, but politically and physically they are out of date and unenforceable and hence are doomed to failure.

A brief look at the history of these efforts will help to illustrate. The United Nations passed a Partition Plan for Palestine in 1947. That plan was rejected by the Arabs and accepted by the Jews. The war of 1948 left Israel in control of an area almost one-third larger than that allocated by the Plan. The war also left several hundred thousand Arabs in refugee status. After the war the United Nations passed a resolution upholding the Partition Plan in order to avoid endorsing territorial acquisition by means of war. The resolution also recognized the right of the Palestinians to repatriation or just compensation. The spirit of that resolution has been reasserted again and again by the United Nations and for the same reasons: to avoid giving legitimacy to war gains. Israel claims, in the words of its spokesman Aba Eban, that the Partition Plan was voided by the war and that an egg broken years ago cannot be reconstructed. The Partition Plan is dead. The United Nations has done next to nothing to force implementation and has no courage to modify that resolution. How can we expect Israel to abide by a resolution that is not to its advantage when hardly any pressure is placed on it to do so? On the other hand, how can we expect the Arabs to forego a moral weapon, the United Nations resolution, which puts them in the right and which, in principle, condemns the actions of Israel? By upholding this out-of-date resolution the United Nations may have contributed to the impasse which has characterized the Arab-Israeli conflict ever since.

The next major United Nations peace plan followed the 1967 war, which left Israel with a vast area in addition to its prewar territory. The United Nations reaffirmed its stand against territorial gains through war and called on Israel to withdraw from the territories occupied in the recent conflict; it also reaffirmed the right of all states in the Middle East to live in peace and insisted on an end to belligerency; it affirmed further the necessity of guaranteeing freedom of navigation through international waterways, territorial inviolability, and the need to promote a peaceful settlement, including the establishment of demilitarized zones. A just settlement of the refugee problem remains an integral part of the United Nations resolution. The United Nations has in a sense shifted the emphasis to the 1967 war gains and to withdrawal from the newly occupied territories only. That would leave Israel with the war gains realized in 1948. This implies that only the most recent gains of war must be nullified. By implication, if Israel expands still further, the 1967 gains would no longer be subject to condemnation by the United Nations.

Obviously the United Nations will not admit this, although this is exactly what is happening. Furthermore, the United Nations is calling for a just settlement of the refugee problem. A just settlement is vague and allows for all kinds of interpretation by both sides when in fact the United Nations knows that repatriation is no longer feasible nor even advisable, although it might still be considered a just settlement. By refraining from a face-to-face confrontation with reality, in the name of international diplomacy, the United Nations has left a wide area of uncertainty within which the conflict is nourished and hatred is deepened.

It is apparent that the United Nations has moved away from the 1948 resolution, but the language of the new resolution does not definitively indicate this shift. The United Nations has continued to rely on moral persuasion, which has left little impact on either side and has therefore failed to bring about peace. Whether the United Nations can be more effective is another matter and will be treated below. It is sufficient at this point to observe that the United Nations resolutions have sustained a condition of uncertainty, irresponsibility, and even conflict. Neither party has seen fit to put an end to its immoral contribution to the conflict, and each regards the United Nations a supporter of its claims to justice and sovereignty. It is true that the United Nations has been most effective in bringing about ceasefires, which is a great achievement; peace, however, is another matter.

V

There have been other peace proposals which are not official but which deserve attention as potential alternatives, although they may have failed to materialize. Each of these plans has been presented from a point of view that often has invited objections from one party or the other. This presentation is intended mainly to illustrate the complexity of the situation and the failure of reason, relative to emotion and irrationality, in reacting to peace proposals.

In 1958, Erskine B. Childers wrote an article, "Impasse in the Holy Land,"[18] in which he emphasized three key issues

[18]Ernest B. Childers, "Impasse in the Holy Land," *Encounter*, vol. XI, no.1, July 1958, pp. 46–66.

in peace negotiations: Jewish immigration and Arab fears of Israeli expansion; territorial differences; and the Arab refugees. Childers proposed a restriction on immigration as a precondition to any peaceful settlement; such self-imposed restrictions would be accompanied by readiness of other countries to receive Jewish immigrants should the need for that arise. Once this precondition had been satisfied, Childers proposes demilitarization of the Negev under a joint Arab-Israeli-United Nations administration, resettlement of the refugees in the Negev, and that Elath be declared a free port for Israel in return for making Haifa a free port for Jordan. Other details are mainly elaborations of these points. The plan obviously was condemned by Israel because it infringed on the sovereignty of Israel by interfering with the policy on immigration. Israel has held the territory in question for a decade, has won another battle which brought its forces to the banks of the Suez Canal, and has opened its gates to all Jews, wherever they are. A plan that infringed on these positions was bound to be rejected. It was, and Childers was attacked as biased against the Jews.

A more recent and comprehensive plan has been advanced by John C. Campbell, presumably as a blueprint for the United States policy in the Middle East. This plan is important because of its timing and because it takes Soviet interests in the Middle East into consideration. The plan is based on the following points:

(1) Arab acceptance of Israel as a sovereign state and Israeli withdrawal to agreed state frontiers described below, set forth in binding obligations (the two points being inseparabley linked but with some flexibility in timing to make it easier for both sides to carry them out).

(2) State frontiers to be the lines of June 4, 1967, with certain specific exceptions: minor adjustments in the border between Israel

and the West Bank (whether the latter is Jordan or Arab Palestine); special international status for East Jerusalem, the detailed legal and other aspects of which would be left to consideration among the many parties concerned; special status for the Gaza strip (e.g. U. N. administration) for a period of ten years; the Golan Heights to be returned to Syria, but only after Syrian acceptance of the U. N. resolution of November 1967 and of the other points of settlement.

(3) Demilitarized zones on both sides of the frontiers, including total demilitarization of the Golan Heights, the Gaza Strip, and the Sharm-el-Sheikh area; U. N. observers and peacemaking forces in all demilitarized zones, subject to withdrawal only with the consent of the Security Council.

(4) Acceptance of Israel's right to navigate the Suez Canal and the Strait of Tiran on a basis of equality with other states.

(5) Recognition of the right of the Arab people of Palestine to existence as a nation and to compensation for their privations as refugees, within the framework of a peace settlement as outlined here, but with no unlimited right of return to Israel.

(6) International guarantees of the settlement within the framework of which there would be a U. S. guarantee to Israel."[19]

Will this plan work? It is too early to evaluate its impact, but we can at least estimate its potential for acceptance. The plan has come probably two decades too late for rational consideration by the parties to the conflict.Too much enmity and distrust have accumulated for acceptance of such a plan. Israel has little trust in international guarantees and demilitarization as means of security. The Arabs will have struggled for more than two decades and will have realized no gains or even assured compensation to show for it. In fact, the plan in general is a boon to Israel and a serious compromise for the Arabs. For instance, Israel will gain recognition, peace, secure borders, freedom of navigation, and no Arab refugees. In addition to their losses of 1948, the Arabs will have to

[19]John C. Campbell, "The Arab-Israeli Conflict: An American Policy," FOREIGN AFFAIRS, Oct. 1970, pp. 60–61.

surrender all the above to Israel as well as give up sovereignty over vast areas which they held prior to 1967, including the Gaza Strip, East Jerusalem, the Golan Heights, and Sharm-el-Sheikh. Furthermore, the Palestinian Arabs are asked to give up any rights of return to their homes for simple compensation for their privations as refugees. What do the Arabs get in return? They will be assured of Israeli withdrawal from the territory they occupied in the war and a safe conduct agreement from Israel. Needless to say, this policy is too one-sided to be accepted by one of the two main parties to the conflict. To adopt it as a policy, the United States would be supporting the charge that it does not really care to promote peace, which would leave the Soviet Union a free hand in the area and which would open the Suez Canal for Soviet ships en route to the Indian Ocean. One wonders whether the proponents of this plan actually envisaged its adoption when for all practical purposes the potential for its acceptance by the Arabs is virtually nil. The only hope it offers is that it may be a good starting point for deliberation, with a certain degree of commitment by the United States, in seeking a settlement. The end result, however, remains a remote prospect.

VI

These various approaches to peace have been doomed in part because they were one-sided, unrealistic, or simply not meant to promote a settlement. Their proponents either failed to look at the views of all the warring parties or simply chose to ignore some of them. These proposals have always remained close to traditional diplomacy tactics, which permit hiding the facts, masking the intentions, and explaining away all suffering as the price for an ultimate victory. This has been the case even when no victory could be anticipated and no gains were possible to attain. These peace plans could not have succeeded mostly because they were highly unrealistic and impractical and neither side expected them to succeed.

Chapter 4	The Future Can Still Be Bright:
	Another Peace Proposal!

It is probably presumptuous to propose another peace plan and think of it as the panacea for the ills in the Middle East. The problem is not caused by a lack of proposals or of peace plans. The failure in settling the conflict is more the result of the uncooperative and unrealistic attitudes assumed by the warring parties and of the complications brought about by the cold-war policies of the major powers. The failure is also the result of the slow-moving procedures and diplomatic maneuvers of national and international bodies, which are ordinarily useful in hedging against premature decisions. In the present situation these delaying tactics have been harmful to both sides in that they allow military reorganization and rearming to take place. Before presenting another peace plan, I should like to focus attention on what I have described as the *unrealistic* positions of the two main parties to the conflict. I suggest that unless realism is restored, a peace settlement can only be forced on one or the other party and therefore is bound to be an unstable settlement. On the other hand, once a certain degree of realism has been restored, sacrifices by both sides will become meaningful, and a stable settlement will become possible. Let us look at these unrealistic attitudes and how they can be modified.

I

The Arabs should recognize the following points:
a) Israel is a reality. It is a sovereign state. It is politically and socially viable and is economically at least as viable as any of the Arab states. To continue to deny its existence and to refer to its domain as Occupied Palestine—especially in the Arabic press—is childish. To withhold diplomatic recognition is one thing but to deny the mere existence of a state is quite different and actually meaningless. This Arab policy toward Israel is similar to the former U. S. policy of nonrecognition of Communist China, which not only did not hurt China at all but actually benefited it. By withholding recognition of China and by blocking its admission to the United Nations, China was spared the responsibility entailed by diplomatic relations with other countries and by membership in the United Nations. The U. S. has finally changed its position and China is a member of the United Nations, but many years of possible Chinese cooperation have been lost forever.

The unfortunate impact of the Arab position with respect to Israel is that large numbers of Arab people take it seriously and use it to sustain other unrealistic and harmful policies or actions. For example, to see college students refusing to use a map because it identifies Israel as a nation is almost unbelievable, especially when Israel is a member of the United Nations and has diplomatic relations with more than one hundred other nations. This happens with disturbing frequency. It is time that the Arabs face the reality of Israel and behave accordingly and maturely.

This common unrealistic approach to the national status of

Israel among the Arabs is also significant as a reflection of inconsistencies in the behavior of Arab leaders and Arab spokesmen. Apparently attitudes and language that deny the existence of Israel are meant only for local mass consumption and for sustaining mass support and appeasing emotions; communication with international diplomatic agencies and the international press acknowledge the existence of Israel, regardless of diplomatic recognition. This double standard in regard to the mere existence of Israel is unhealthy and may, in fact, have reached a point where the mass of Palestinian Arabs feel that there has been a sell-out to Israel and the United States by certain Arab leaders. Realism would dictate clarity and consistency in referring to Israel as a reality and as a sovereign national entity.

b) It is equally unrealistic to think that Israel can be destroyed as a state, either by wishing it out of existence or by war, at least not in the foreseeable future. Israel is strong, and the Arabs are weak. The security of Israel derives from the highly supportive international attitude toward it. None of the big powers and few, if any, of the small powers would condone or permit actions that would destroy Israel. They would back up Israel not because they are against the Arabs, which may be the case in certain instances, but because Israel represents the salvation of a people that has suffered immensely. They would back up Israel also because any attempt to destroy that state would be a threat to the international community which guarantees sovereignty to all nations. In addition, Israel has enough supporters to influence the policies of the big powers and make sure that Israel is there to stay. Even the Soviet Union cannot be expected to condone the destruction of the State of Israel; Soviet Russia was one of the first nations to recognize that state *de jure* in 1948. Soviet policy has been expedient enough to invite uncertainty; should the tide change a little, Israel might find herself protected by the Eastern bloc, as was the case in 1948 and for several years thereafter.

It is also unrealistic to think of destroying Israel by war without the risk of a third world war in which the two superpowers would be involved. It would be difficult to exaggerate the degree of U. S. commitment to Israel. The President of the United States has consistently made statements to that effect. When it became apparent about two years ago that the U.S. government might pressure Israel to make concessions toward a settlement, more than two-thirds of the U.S. Senators sought reassurance from the Secretary of State that no such pressure would be applied and that the security of Israel would not be endangered. The Secretary of State obliged. At the same time, there is little reason to believe that Soviet Russia would risk a world war in order to subdue Israel or to please the Arabs. The Arabs would be politically immature if many thought that they would be allowed to march into Israel and occupy it while the world stood by idly. The history of the conflict certainly points against such a possibility. Therefore, any gains in the conflict against Israel must be realized by other alternatives which are not predicated on the destruction of that state.

c) It is time that the Arabs stop their wishful thinking about subduing Israel by economic boycott. The boycott itself has not been successful, and there have been rumors that some Arab countries have taken the initiative to trade with Israel through third parties. Even if Arab policies were more thoroughly implemented, there is little reason to believe that an Arab boycott would harm Israel enough to undermine its economic viability as a state or to force an agreement on it. Israel depends on outside resources which can hardly be influenced by the boycott. The Israeli economy has succeeded in finding markets despite the boycott. Indeed, one might wonder whether Jordan, Tunisia, Morocco, or Syria are anymore viable than Israel. Israel so far has shown that it can withstand the boycott for many more years, or even indefinitely, as long as it can depend on outside support, and that support seems guaranteed. The Arabs have blacklisted hundreds of companies which trade with Israel. They also have blacklisted artists, journalists, and even tourists who openly visit Israel. The negative impact on Israel has been virtually nil. The boycott has often led to a concerted effort to defend Israel and to give it added support to offset the imaginary effects of the boycott. The boycott helped to rally well-intended people to defend the seeming underdog, Israel, and provided ammunition for propaganda against the Arabs. The resources expended on the abortive boycott could have been much more efficiently utilized in other areas. Arab economists should have been outspoken in this regard, but little has been done to amend the record.

d) Another fad of Arab propaganda, which is totally unrealistic, is that sooner or later Israel will have to give in because of the economic costs of the war. Expenditure on mobilization and the loss of economic activities that are thereby restricted are heavy burdens to the Israeli economy and cannot be borne for long. In actuality the economic burden of the war on Israel has been relatively minor. Not only has the Israeli economy seemed able to withstand the pressure, but much of that pressure has been shifted to outside supporters. The economic burden on Israel can hardly be a threat to the economy, and Arab propaganda on that point is virtually meaningless.

Unfortunately, Arab observers tend to publish data which seem to support that attitude but with little documentation or verification of the sources. It is thought, for example, that the 1967 war was such a burden on Israel that its economy has been suffering ever since. There is little documentation of such results. In fact, the war resolved the problem of unemployment, left little destruction at home since the war was carried onto enemy land, recruited large sums of aid from the outside, and provided Israel with large amounts of booty. To consider the economic impact as a debilitating burden is misleading and definitely indefensible. The Arabs would be building castles in the sand if they were to be guided by such observations.

e) If politically, militarily, or economically the burdens of the war cannot be strong enough to undermine the state of Israel and destroy it, the only other possible way is a war of nerves and a hope that the feeling of insecurity will increase enough to render a settlement highly desirable. This expected psychological impact is groundless. The Jews were living in greater insecurity before they came to Palestine and have been under insecure conditions ever since. Insecurity has almost become a way of life for many of them, and they are able to stand it as a normal condition. The farmer in a border settlement has adjusted to the idea of carrying a gun while working on his farm. He has become convinced that his options are limited, and his inability to stand that insecurity could mean the destruction of his hopes and dreams; he is not about to let that happen. The Arabs might as well understand that and behave accordingly.

f) And if none of these methods is realistic as a means of destroying Israel, it is even less realistic to think of diplomacy and the return of Arab refugees to their homes as the means to do so. The diplomatic defenses favoring Israel will also protect its territorial integrity, at least to preclude the return of Arab refugees to the areas abandoned prior to 1948. However, the Arabs should understand that the return of the refugees to Israel is neither feasible nor even desirable. It is not feasible because of the changes affected in their homes and properties, but more so because any such repatriation is bound to change the political character of the state. The Jews who would like to have a Jewish state will definitely see in repatriation a destruction of their plan. Even for the Arabs themselves, repatriation could mean the creation of a minority problem that has caused havoc in other societies. The Arabs would be well-advised to assume a realistic attitude and seek a settlement which does not stipulate repatriation—not even as a bargaining position. Many Arabs mistake the bargaining tactic for a real objective and become spellbound by the rhetoric of those tactics. That has been quite harmful and ought to be abandoned.

g) The Arabs would be more realistic if they recognized their own weaknesses and mistakes and stopped blaming their failures on others. They should remember that failure to reach a settlement is harming a whole generation of Arabs, much more than it is harming Israel. How long can they stand the pressure is uncertain, but it will not be long. The people are bound to ask why, and the leaders will have no satisfactory answers. Elements of civil war in Jordan are quite evident. The Arabs suffer, and Israel is just a spectator. At least in part these are results of the chronic lack of realism which has characterized Arab attitudes, both of the Arab states and of the Palestinian Arabs.

h) Arab lack of realism, however, extends a little further in setting as a condition for peace the limitation on Jewish immigration into Israel. Arab fears of Zionist expansionism may be real and justified. However it is unrealistic to infringe on the sovereignty of Israel and to demand a restriction on immigration. It is also unrealistic and even meaningless to expect valid assurances from Israel against expansion. Such assurances would be good only as long as Israel wished them to be so. While the Arabs may be playing a diplomatic or political game by sounding an alarm against such expansionism, a realistic defense would be to fortify their own defenses sufficiently to stand any degree of Israeli pressure. In the absence of genuine peace and mutual trust, and given the lack of confidence in international security guarantees, the Arabs have no justification in continuing their unrealistic demands for assurances and for restrictions on immigration. Once the Arabs assume a more realistic attitude, their approach to a settlement is bound to take a new direction which would help to bring an end to the war and to remove the fears of expansionism.

II

Arab lack of realism is easily matched by the lack of realism and reason in the Israeli position. The Israelis seem to believe that they are the chosen people, that they can occupy, expand, and settle on other peoples' land and still be accepted by those same people as peaceful and well-intentioned neighbors. This arrogance extends to the agency which legitimated the existence of Israel. Israel is willing to accept support from the international bodies that voted for its creation but is unwilling to respect the opinions of those same bodies with regard to the war with the Arabs. The Israeli leaders insist on having the cake and eating it too. Let me illustrate:

(1) It is unrealistic that Israel insist that it is only seeking a national home or refuge as originally envisaged and still adopt a policy of militarism and occupation. Refuge implies a good-neighbor policy. It implies tolerance and cooperation with others. Israel has shown none of these qualities to its neighbors. To shift the blame to the other party is itself unrealistic since Israel has changed the mission of the early Zionists who indeed were seeking a home and a refuge. When Nahum Goldman reminded the Jews of these contradictions, he was openly attacked by Israeli leaders.

(2) Israel denies any expansionist intentions, but the history of Israel has been one of expansionism. Israel has given no evidence of nonexpansionist convictions; the contrary has been more true. The acquisitions of the 1948 war have been retained and settled; the acquisitions of 1967 have been retained and partly settled. All Israeli policy declarations tend to lead to the same conclusion: Israel will retain territorial gains from the 1967 war as it did after 1948. It is unrealistic to expect the Arabs to believe the claims for nonexpansionist coexistence. It is incumbent upon Israel to give evidence of their good intentions and of their nonexpansionist commitments, not only by words but also by actions.

(3) Israel insists on direct negotiation, peace agreement, comprehensive settlement, and no predetermined conditions. Israel should know, however, that an imposed peace settlement is bound to be unstable. To force the Arabs to comply and to sign an agreement can hardly be called a peace. Furthermore, it is ridiculous to stress procedural matters if agreements on substance can be reached by other means.

Israel may be seeking a moral victory, since the military victory has proved insufficient, by gaining recognition from the Arabs through direct negotiations. Israel is using a psychology which applies very well to the Middle East and especially to the Arabs. To admit the existence of Israel by negotiating would be a victory for Israel and a surrender for the Arabs. Israel is actually seeking to humiliate the Arabs even further by adding moral defeat to the military defeat. A realistic policy which seeks coexistence and possibly cooperation would try to avoid taking advantage of the opponent by humiliating him more than absolutely necessary. Israel is putting the Arabs in a position that leaves no alternative but to refuse direct negotiation and moral defeat. Israeli leaders ought to know the psychology of the Middle Eastern Arabs and try to work with them with as little injury to their pride or self-respect as possible. That would suggest maturity and realism.

(4) Israel has been carrying on a campaign against withdrawal from the occupied territories on the basis of their need for secure borders. Occupation of the Golan Heights, the Sinai, and Sharm-el-Sheikh apparently will guarantee secure borders. Israel knows very well that modern weapons have obviated any border security provided by such natural defenses. They may be guarantees against old-fashioned or poorly equipped armies, but modern warfare cannot be prevented by such borders. Israel has used this argument because the advantages of holding on to territory seem to be in its favor, even though that same argument seems to be a hindrance to a negotiated settlement. Israel's inflexibility on this point has almost created antagonism between U. S. Secretary of State Rogers and the Israeli leaders. Secretary Rogers has emphasized the significance of political agreements as sources of security, rather than natural borders as its source. Israeli leaders were upset because that would imply withdrawal and loss of territory. If security is the main objective, Israel should be willing to entertain alternative ways of guaranteeing security. Insisting on territorial occupation suggests territorial greed rather than the search for security.

(5) Israel has made a number of unrealistic assumptions or claims. For example, Israelis think that time is on their side, that attrition is in their favor, and that the Arabs are bound to get tired, burdened, and therefore more willing to settle the conflict peacefully. These assumptions are false. The Arabs have internal and external resources which seem adequate to continue the war of attrition. The Arab states feel little insecurity, and reports from large Arab population centers suggest that the war has had little impact on daily life.

Why should the Arabs, then, be willing to surrender and sign a peace treaty without concessions from Israel?

Another mistaken Israeli assumption is that Israel has military superiority and therefore does not need to make any concessions. Such superiority is bound to diminish. The Arabs, starting from a low level of expertise, have no way to go but upward in improving their technology and military ability. They are bound to narrow or even close the gap sometime in the future and given their numbers, Israeli superiority can hardly be regarded as more than a short-run phenomenon; it is unrealistic to regard such superiority as inherent or everlasting. An equally significant fact is that the Palestinian guerrillas can move only in one direction—to become better organized, more desperate, and therefore more of a menace to Israel than they have been. They have nothing more to lose, and any benefits they can realize will be a great incentive to continue guerrilla activities. To consider the Palestinians as secondary to the conflict and to depend on King Hussein to control them is self-defeating; these are the people who have been badly injured, and they are the ones who will cause damage and create insecurity for Israel unless they are gratified. To ignore their potential for sabotage and destruction is almost unbelievable, especially for Israeli Jews who have realized their objectives partly by these same means.

(6) A different, though equally misleading, claim is that Israel can contribute to the welfare of the Arab countries if given the chance through a peace settlement. It is claimed that trade and aid would be quite valuable. These are highly unjustifiable claims. Israel has nothing to offer which the Arabs cannot secure more cheaply somewhere else. The Arabs have a market and do not need the Israeli market either to sell or to buy. They can get the aid they want from

other countries, including the western powers, the United Nations, Russia, and China, at the lowest possible costs to themselves. Israel has little to offer that is unique or indispensable.

Actually Israel might be considered an economic threat to the developing Arab economies, should an open-trade policy be established. If the Arab market were open to Israel, it is possible that many Arab producers would be forced out of the market. Although such a development might be beneficial to the region as a whole, it can be destructive to the individual producers and to the national interests of the country to which they belong. It is true that in an atmosphere of cooperation such fears need not be serious, but it is unrealistic for Israel to ignore such fears and to brag about possible contributions to the Arab economies. Such assumptions and beliefs tend to be misleading and unhelpful to the cause of a settlement.

(7) Finally, it is unrealistic to expect peace "at no price." Peace may not be a salable commodity, but it is not a free good either. It involves transactions of benefits and entails costs. At what price, or at what cost, would certain benefits be justified? To insist that Israel be accepted as it is may be good rhetoric, but it is an unrealistic position to assume if peace is indeed sought after. It is more helpful for Israel to face these facts and to act accordingly to promote that badly needed peace and security. The mere fact that there can be negotiations suggests that a form of transaction will take place. Every transaction implies a price or a cost, and thus a negotiated settlement or peace would imply a cost. Israel may be correct in insisting on being accepted as it is in principle, but it is practical and realistic to suggest alternative ways for securing such acceptance; these alternative ways would represent the price for peace.

III

If both the Arabs nations and Israel agree to be more realistic and less concerned with procedural and diplomatic tactics, there is a good chance that a settlement can be concluded. I should like to outline a plan that requires sacrifices but which is sufficiently practical to lead to a solution if there is any good will left on both sides. The plan is based on the following premises:

(1) Matters of substance will take priority over matters of form and procedure. Whether negotiations are direct or indirect is unimportant if negotions can be carried out at all. Whether an agreement is called a peace treaty, a nonaggression treaty, or even an indefinite ceasefire, it should make little difference, and such an arrangement should be welcome. The assumption is that other steps will follow in the future.

(2) Peace and harmony cannot be imposed. Nonaggression might be guaranteed, and a ceasefire might be imposed. However, peace, harmony, and friendship must evolve. Any attempts to impose such agreements have the potential of failing and the agreements thereby concluded, of being quickly broken.

(3) War gains cannot be legitimized by de facto occupation. The failure to return war acquisitions can hardly promote peaceful arrangements. Any war gains that cannot possibly be returned must be so declared by a third party and compensated for in full, at least to the satisfaction of an arbitrator.

(4) A final settlement of all the issues is a difficult operation, and may have many snags. A viable approach would be to seek such a settlement in degrees, according to the priority of issues to be settled. This does not preclude the outlining

of a general settlement plan, but implementation need not depend either on the completion of such a plan or on the feasibility of its total implementation; a partial settlement is better than no settlement at all.

Given these premises, I suggest the following plan.

PLACE OF ISRAEL IN THE REGION

(1) The Arab states and the Palestinian guerrillas will acknowledge the existence of Israel as a sovereign nation in the region and one which cannot be ignored as a neighbor and as a member of the international community of nations. This declaration does not constitute a formal recognition, but it is a step toward removing the unrealism inherent in denying the existence of the state. Obviously such a declaration could smooth the way toward peaceful coexistence.

(2) Concurrent with the Arab declaration, Israel will declare its intent of being a Middle Eastern state and of wanting to be a peaceful and good neighbor. Israel will also declare its firm commitment to a policy of nonexpansionism, regardless of the possible temptations to expand at the expense of its neighbors.

(3) Both parties will declare their interest in resolving all problems in a framework of peaceful coexistence. They will also promise to keep outside influences or interventions to a minimum. Accordingly, both parties will declare that neither party will seek relations with an outside power that will undermine the other party. This will be an attempt to isolate the conflict from the intricacies and immoralities of the cold war.

This set of declarations is a preliminary step which affirms the often-made statements by all parties that they are interested in peace. These declarations mean only a commitment to the idea of peaceful coexistence. All other matters will be handled within that framework. A peace treaty, if at all possible, should have a chance to evolve after contacts have been made and certain problems resolved.

These proposals will serve several objectives and are indispensible if coexistence is to take place. The Arabs will face reality and admit it to themselves and to the world and thus remove a psychological handicap and a mask that has been blinding their minds and thoughts about the Middle East political complex. At the same time, Israel will commit itself within the same context to peaceful nonexpansionist coexistence. The degree to which these commitments will be meaningful and binding will depend on the follow-up arrangements which would make coexistence feasible. Furthermore, once these declarations have been made, the general atmosphere is bound to change toward a more positive and viable search for a settlement. In other words, these declarations will help to create a moral and psychological environment that would be consistent with, and possibly conducive to, such a settlement. In the absence of such declarations, neither party can be expected to pursue a settlement with optimism, trust, or commitment.

The Arab Refugees

The present approach is pragmatic. This is a problem which needs to be resolved at the least cost and by means which avoid new problems for otherwise settled communities, whether Arab or Jew. In this perspective, Israel will *honor* the right of the Palestinian Arabs to be repatriated to their homes as a matter of human understanding and, to an extent, of justice. Israel will explain from its standpoint the impracticality of such repatriation, given that Arab homes have been altered and new people have been settled in them. As an alternative, Israel will undertake to cooperate fully in finding new homes that would satisfy the Palestinians as the next best alternative to repatriation.

In their turn, the Palestinians will accept the judgment that repatriation is impractical, though they need not forsake their right to it. The Palestinians will agree that even though they may have the right to return, according to certain criteria, the immediate obstacles as well as the long-term potentials for trouble preclude the enforcement of that right. Hence, they will agree to seek an alternative. Among the policies to recommend in this respect are the following:

(a) Full compensation for land and property to all those who have been dislocated by the Arab-Israeli war. The compensation will include overhead payments to compensate for the public (community) losses in addition to the private losses.

(b) Israel, the Arab countries, and the international community of nations will pool funds for compensation to be dispensed under joint administration.

(c) The Palestinian Arabs will determine their own political future, as individuals and as a group. They will decide whether they will become a part of Jordan, whether they will form a Palestinian state in the eastern part of Palestine, whether they will settle in the Arab countries, or whether they will emigrate out of the region. They obviously will have the option of combining alternatives in the sense that some of them may choose to go their own way to begin a new life. The Palestinian Arabs will also determine the kind of relationship they choose to promote with Israel and with the Arab countries in the future. Until such determination has been made, the Palestinian Arabs will assume autonomy under the protection of the Arab League or the United Nations.

(d) The international community will ensure that the

Palestinians who are willing to emigrate in and out of the region will be given priorities and the facilities to do so, both as individuals and as groups. Some may wish to emigrate to Canada, the United States, Latin America, or New Zealand, and legal facilities should be made available.

(e) Those who desire to settle in the Arab countries will be allowed to do so and their cost of resettlement (travel and overhead in the case of groups) will be borne by Israel and the international community as compensation and as a problem-solving mechanism. Groups that choose to resettle as units will have compensation for communal losses in order to establish villages or townships.

The problem of the Arab refugees has usually been approached as a political stalemate. I would like to approach it as only a difficult problem which can still be resolved. This plan gives the Arabs a moral victory without inflicting a defeat on Israel. Israel will admit an obligation, and the Arabs will cooperate by recognizing the obstacles in the way of repatriation. Once that has been accomplished, the problem is mainly organizational. The refugees will decide where to resettle and will choose the political system they wish to establish. Obviously, this requires cooperation from Jordan and from the international community, especially if many refugees wish to emigrate. There are many indications that large numbers of Arab families prefer to leave the Middle East and settle in the Western hemisphere. There are indications also that young Arabs have already been leaving the Middle East and prefer not to return. Cooperation from the West and from Jordan would make the problem solvable, while Israel will carry the cost.

This plan will also serve the course of justice by redeeming the losses of all Arabs and Jews who have been dislocated by the war, even those who are not considered refugees.

Material compensation thus will accompany the moral victory which is basic to this plan, not to one party only but to both.

THE BOUNDARIES

The premise in determining boundaries is two-fold: It will be determined independently of war gains and will be rationally determined according to a meaningful set of criteria, such as population distribution, contiguity, and access to the outside world. The proposed arrangement is the following:

(1) Israel will declare that all territorial war gains are returnable, including those acquired in 1948. Only those boundaries determined by the United Nations will be *bona fide* boundaries of the sovereign state. To allow any other boundaries will entail chaos and provide the Arabs with the rationale for continuing to fight a war against Israel with the objective of readjusting the borders.

(2) Israel will request, and the United Nations will agree to redefine those boundaries to render them consistent with the demands for legitimacy and rationality. Both the Arabs and Israelis will accept these redefined boundaries, even though they may conflict with their full expectations.

(3) The United Nations will also create safeguards against border conflicts by demilitarizing or controlling certain areas, if deemed advisable. This will help to reduce but will not eliminate border insecurity. The people themselves must do the rest to assure security; for example, promote good will, abide by coexistence, and try to rebuild what has been in ruins for two decades.

(4) Population centers affected by redefined boundaries will have the same right to determine their own political future as the other Palestinian Arabs. For example, the peo-

ple of Gaza, Jerusalem, or other places subject to redefinition will have an option regarding their future.

(5) Jerusalem, both the Old and the New cities, will fall in the area whose status is subject to redefinition. The United Nations may reaffirm the resolution on internationalization or propose a new status for the city to fit the new circumstances. It might choose to designate Jerusalem as a free city and headquarters of the United Nations.

This boundary proposal will serve the causes of security and also nonexpansionism. Once Israel has committed itself to nonexpansionism, these boundaries become fully consistent with the idea of peaceful coexistence. The questions of practicality and of security may be handled within this framework. Where complete withdrawal is impractical, adjustment will be made accordingly.

The question of security can easily be exaggerated. In the present state of technology, there are no natural boundaries that may be considered secure. Security must be an added or man-made feature, and the United Nations and the big powers can play a role in this respect. In the final analysis, security must be an outgrowth of peaceful coexistence and of abiding by the formal agreements. All other considerations must either be justified by the international community, such as the status of Jerusalem, or be handled in accordance with the policy of nonexpansionism.

INTERNATIONAL WATERWAYS

National sovereignty must be guaranteed to all nations and not to some only.

(1) International waterways in the area will be open to all nations equally but not so as to threaten the sovereignty or security of the state in whose domain such waterways exist.

The Suez Canal and the Straits of Tiran are in the domain of Egypt. These will be open to commercial and peaceful usage at all times and to all nations.

(2) In case of military conflict, Egypt will restrict these waterways against military usage which might endanger its own security. Any other arrangement will simply be meaningless and cannot hold.

(3) War material that might endanger the security of the waterways themselves or of Egypt will be subject to regulation by Egypt. This arrangement is merely a pragmatic arrangement since most agreements are usually voided by the war in any case. However it does constitute recognition of the rights and of the sovereignty of the nations in the region.

The question of waterways can be highly complicated by international jurisdictional agreements and conventions. It would be a great oversimplification to expect any country to permit enemy forces passage through its waterways if these would endanger its own security. Only a weak country would allow that and only by failing to prevent it out of weakness. The Suez Canal can and should be open to all navigation, but in time of war Egypt can hardly be expected to allow enemy vessels through; when forced to do so, Egypt blocked the canal. A pragmatic approach would have to respect national security demands and promote good will to preclude war possibilities. The above proposal does that.

THE ARABS OF ISRAEL

Although not facing a major problem at present, the fate of the Arabs of Israel is not fully or harmoniously settled. Their problems are largely dormant but will not remain so forever. To avoid future conflicts, they should have the option of making their own decisions, like the other Palestinians, in addition to the option of staying as a small minority within the state of Israel. Should they choose to stay, it must be clear to what extent they may seek autonomy or integration in the Israeli society. They should also be made aware of the degree to which autonomy or integration can be meaningfully realized. In any case, they should have the choice and make the decision regarding their future.

This plan may seem too simple to be helpful. It does, however, touch on all the relevant aspects of the conflict. Its main strengths are as follows: It takes into consideration questions of cultural importance such as admission of responsibility, forgiveness, and face-saving, which are ego-inflating in the Middle Eastern culture. It permits a high degree of flexibility to accommodate the desires of both groups, as these desires are reconciled by a friendly encounter between the two parties based on coexistence. The plan allows a certain degree of gradualism of implementation of agreed-upon solutions so that mistakes can be corrected as they come up and a trial-and-error process can be utilized. It also restores to the Palestinian Arabs a certain degree of self-respect, self-determination, and independence consistent with the rehabilitation philosophy applied to the Jewish people who came to Israel. Finally, the plan recognizes the predicament of the Arabs of Israel who have so far been left out of all other proposals for a peaceful settlement. No doubt implementation is not easy, but with determination it can be done, and the results will be mutually satisfying to the warring parties, if only they try.

Chapter 5

Where the Responsibility Lies:
Reflections on the Future

Twenty-four years have passed since Israel came into existence and the Palestinian Arabs became refugees. We are
little closer to a settlement now than at any other time in the
past, statements to the contrary by various world diplomats
and politicians not withstanding. Gunnar Jarring is still trying, but even his initiative has recently come under attack as
an obstacle to peace; he was accused of promising the Arabs
more than Israel is willing to give up. The United States
continues to sound optimistic, although it continues to send
reassurances and arms to Israel. Soviet Russia is supposed to
have become more interested in a settlement than previously but continues to build an arsenal in Egypt and other
Arab countries, while allowing emigration of Soviet Jews to
Israel. The Arab countries and Israel continue to issue statements and declarations dedicated to peace with their neighbors, but little action follows to prove their intentions. In the
meantime, the Palestinian guerrillas are becoming better
organized and probably more effective in fighting their war.
There is a danger that they may have reached a degree of
self-deception that allows them to think that they can pre-

vent a peaceful settlement or that they can recover the territory occupied by Israel on their own by war. If so, the future can indeed be gloomy and peace only a dream. I prefer to be a little more optimistic and look forward to a political settlement and to peaceful coexistence.

Sooner or later the war between the Arab countries and Israel will come to an end; wars have always come to an end. It is the cost of delaying that end which matters. By delaying a permanent settlement costs will continue to be incurred in various forms. Some costs will be in the form of scars which may never be erased. There is little doubt that a settlement is possible; many plans already have been proposed, and I have added another. So far the signs of a settlement are too few and too uncertain to generate optimism. Who is responsible for this state of affairs and how can we get out of it?

In their search for peace the American Friends (Quakers) appealed to the United Nations and the Big Four; they also appealed to the Israelis, to the Arab States, to the Palestinian Arabs, to Jordan, to the leaders of the American Jewish Community, to the U.S. Congress, to the White House, to the Department of State, and to the world community. Their appeal asked these bodies to continue the search for peace and to reassess their own positions on the conflict.[20] This is a comprehensive list of appeals which can hardly be surpassed. I am not in a position to send out appeals. I should like to focus attention on some steps that need to be taken by the external forces and by the warring parties. The Arabs and Israelis are the two peoples who, in the final analysis, are responsible for war and for peace. They are the potential winners or losers; they are the parties that will be scarred by this immoral and unending war.

[20]For American Friends peace position: See *Search for Peace in the Middle East* (Greenwich, Conn.: Fawcett Publications, Inc., 1970).

I

The external forces I am concerned with are three: the
United Nations, the foreign powers which extend economic
and military aid to the warring parties, and the other foreign
countries which extend moral support to one or the other of
these parties and thus complicate matters and possibly delay
settlement. The United Nations' responsibility is grave and
dubious. The impact of the United Nations is unmistakable
if its policies can be carried out, but given the structure of
that agency, it is dubious whether it can be any more effective or better directed toward peace than it has been. As a
collection of members with individual sovereignties, the
United Nations can succeed only if enough good will is shown
by the members. Nevertheless, the United Nations owes it to
the cause of peace and harmony to recognize what can and
what cannot be done and to take a position accordingly. The
United Nations may be unable to enforce certain resolutions,
but it can modify these resolutions and bring them as close
to reality as possible. For example, the United Nations owes
it to the Palestinian Arabs to tell them whether a resolution
for their repatriation is still meaningful. If its conclusion is
that it is not, the United Nations owes it to those same Arabs
and to the Arab states and Israel to say so and to modify that
resolution to make it relevant and realistic. By such dyna-
mism the United Nations will remove a moral obstacle
against a settlement of the refugee problem. Indeed, even if
the United Nations by a majority vote still considers repatriation as just and morally right, it owes it to the warring parties
to be practical. It should declare its position regarding justice
and morality, proceed to deal with the practical solution, and
introduce adequate compensatory measures to avoid com-

promising justice. Once that amendment has been made, the Arabs will no longer feel morally right in insisting on repatriation or in avoiding a settlement, and Israel will be obligated to compensate for failing to carry out the original resolution. I am aware of the dangers inherent in this approach. But I am also aware of the effects of the present alternative. The failure to bring about a settlement and the hopelessness of repatriation, without another tragedy, are more harmful than a realistic attempt to face the truth and to modify the United Nations resolution accordingly.

The United Nations is equally and similarly responsible in dealing with the border problem. For all practical purposes, the Partition Plan of 1947 is dead. The Arabs know it and the Israelis know it, but no other set of borders has been designated as the legitimate borders of Israel. The pre-1967 borders were ceasefire borders established at the end of the 1948 war, pending a settlement. As has been noted above, even these borders have now become matters of history. The United Nations owes it to the warring parties to take a position in which it would indicate which borders are consistent with the United Nations' principles and which are practical and relevant for a solution. While the United Nations cannot condone territorial war gains, it must be pragmatic enough to see what can be achieved in nullifying such gains and what cannot. Again the principle of compensation can be usefully applied. In other words, the United Nations owes it to the people of the Middle East to indicate the principles that should be respected and to specify the pragmatic considerations and the practical borders that can be established. If the Partition Plan is dead, let us give it a legal burial; if the 1948 borders are practical borders, they should be made legal; and if they should be modified, the United Nations should proceed to modify them. Each of these policies could carry with it sanctions against violations of the principle. Once the

United Nations has decided to reassess its views of previous resolutions and to modify its position accordingly, a big stumbling block in the way of a settlement will have been removed.

II

The second set of responsibilities falls on those countries which feed the war in the Middle East by giving aid, loans, arms, and political support to one party or the other as a matter of "commitment." The sad aspect of this dilemma is that aid is often conceived as a humanitarian gesture, even though it may be sustaining an unnecessary war. The United States, Britain, France, and Soviet Russia are the most responsible in this regard. Their economic aid, in one form or another, has been accompanied by a replacement fund which offsets any losses of arms or equipment, regardless how little needed these arms are. Thus, when Israel loses planes, the United States assures all the parties concerned that the balance of power must be maintained and therefore Israel must be given additional planes. The Soviet Union immediately races to offset Arab losses in a similar fashion. The latest available count shows that Egypt has 220 MIG 21s, 206 MIG 17s and 15s, and 120 SUIs, in addition to 360 SA2 and 120 SA3 launchers. Israel has just acquired 150 F4 and A4 fighter bombers, in addition to the 220 French-built jets they had before.[21]

Are the United States and the Soviets really concerned only about security? Or are they fighting their own cold war and testing their own weapons in the Middle East? If, as they say, the United States and Soviet Russia, and even Britain and

[21] *Sacramento Bee*, Mr. 22, 1971.

France, are genuinely concerned with a settlement, the first thing they could do is to revamp their arms-shipment policies and search for new approaches. For example, both parties can restrict their arms deliveries to strictly defensive weapons—not offensive weapons in the name of defense. They can deliver up-to-date equipment which can be used only defensively, such as the SAMs which are protecting Egypt against Israeli planes. They can also supervise and regulate the use of these weapons or not deliver them at all. In the final analysis it may be more viable to undertake the defense of the borders directly than to deliver arms and let the warring parties continue their immoral war. The balance of power concept and the replacement fund idea are dangerous; they have been abused and have by necessity contributed to the continuation of the war in the Middle East. These foreign powers may have interests in the Middle East and may be deeply involved in the cold war, but they can serve these objectives without the Arabs and Israelis killing each other. The economic interests of the West can be served better in peace than in war; they will have more resources to expend on the cold war if the hot war comes to an end. And their interests would be better served by befriending the Arabs, as well as the Israelis, than if they maintained the present state of distrust. The Eastern bloc would also have less demands on their resources for aid and would have more chances to spread their ideology, if that is what they are after.

The arms-producing powers also have extended moral and political support to the warring parties. In fact, they have influenced the position taken by the United Nations, mainly to serve their own interests. Yet, they have not had the courage to tell their clients in the Middle East that those interests can be accomplished without war. They have not put pressure on them to be more realistic in their approach to a settlement. Neither Israel nor the Arab countries would be able to carry out a war or sustain their living standards without outside aid. Had the United States and Soviet Russia been genuinely concerned with a settlement, they would soon have made it difficult for Arabs and Israelis to go on fighting. Even without imposing on them a peace settlement, they would bring about some kind of agreement by forcing them to seek one. If the Arabs and Israelis do not have the economic and military means to fight, their only alternative would be to seek a solution through other means; and even if such a solution were not immediately forthcoming, the costs of delaying a settlement would be less than if there were a war. These external powers have the responsibility to spare their allies the agonies of war; they have the responsibility to make the United Nations a more effective instrument of peace; they have the responsibility to their own people not to squander large amounts of capital on nonproductive investment such as war in the Middle East; and they have the responsibility to those millions of Arabs and Jews who are suffering to spare them the tragic effects of a continuation of an immoral war. By withholding offensive arms and by putting economic pressure on their allies, these foreign powers will increase the prospects of a settlement, or at least reduce the costs of an extended wait for that settlement.

III

Part of the responsibility falls on foreign countries which have allied themselves with the Arab countries or with Israel and given them political and moral support without sufficient appreciation of the position of the other party in the war. Moslem countries, for example, have almost blindly supported the Arabs against Israel, even though the conflict is far from religious. They refrain from recognizing Israel and thus remove themselves as possible mediators to bring about a settlement; and yet they have given little or no aid to the Arabs other than words and misleading policy declarations. Pakistan, for instance, is neither able to nor interested in aiding the Arabs, but it goes on supporting the Arabs' unrealistic arguments so that they are reinforced and the conflict is continued. Iran has taken a middle position: it trades with Israel but will not recognize it formally and pretends to be on the side of the Arabs. Actually Iran does not care one way or the other. Only Turkey, as a Moslem country, has recognized Israel fully and has virtually ignored the Arab-Israel conflict.

India and Yugoslavia have sided with the Arabs partly because of a belief in justice but mostly because Egypt declared itself neutral in the cold war. Thus, the neutralists sided with Egypt or the Arabs against Israel, but they have failed to differentiate between right and wrong in Arab policies. Similarly, Israel has friends who go along with her policies to please the United States, because they are unaware of the Arab position, or because they are genuinely interested in helping Israel. West Germany has taken such a position under the pressure of the United States but with little interest in justice or a settlement.

Whatever the reasons, these countries will undoubtedly continue to take sides and will continue to give support to their allies. They would help their allies more by convincing them to be practical and ready to compromise in the name of peace and a settlement. They would help them by at least hearing the other side, by injecting some realism into the situation, and by trying to remove the misleadingly blind support they have given to one party or the other. Just as the Moslem countries must not go on supporting the Arabs blindly, Jews all over the world must revise their position. They actually are postponing a settlement by their blind aid to Israel. Both the world Moslems and the world Jews have a responsibility to look at the conflict in its broadest possible perspective and act accordingly. If they do so, they certainly will find it to their ally's benefit to be pressured into a settlement.

IV

In spite of the various responsibilities, the main responsibility for peace or settlement lies with the Arabs and Israelis more than with any other party. They win or lose; they die or survive; they are the ones to live with whatever arrangements are made. The leaders, sooner or later, may have to account for their policies, but the people are the ones who immediately suffer the consequences of the ongoing war. It is in this perspective that I regard it the responsibility of the people to expedite the moment of reckoning with their leaders and to pressure them into finding a solution. The time lost cannot be recovered. Generations of youngsters are growing up with scars on their memories because of the miseries suffered in a conflict they had nothing to do with. Arab babies born out of Palestine will have little in their past that would justify postponing the settlement. They will have lost years of peace and happiness, while waiting for things unknown to happen. They will continue to hate Israel because they are brought up and trained to do so; but they will also hate their own leaders and elders for not being honest with them and for not reaching a settlement earlier.

Israeli youngsters are not better protected. To grow up in insecurity and tension and to always be warned of an enemy called Arabs does not lead to a wholesome and peaceful life. Their life will not be free of guilt either. For the Israeli Jewish child to learn that his elders had found a home for him by displacing another child is not pleasant. To know that peace could have been achieved but his country's leaders did not cooperate could be dangerous. And for both Arabs and Jews to find after years of bitterness that they are only fighting for a small piece of real estate when both can somehow be accommodated is utterly incomprehensible.

To avoid these unhappy prospects, both Arabs and Jews in the Middle East owe it to themselves and to humanity to review their policies, to explore peace prospects with honesty and determination, and to make the necessary sacrifices and adjustments before more opportunities for settlement are lost. Let me be more specific by looking at the various Arab countries and Israel and see what lies ahead for them.

Lebanon has never been active against Israel, and there is little reason for the Lebanese to become more involved at the present time. In fact, there is probably an inducement for them to promote a settlement to spare their southern towns and villages the agonies of falling prey to the Palestinians on one side and the Israelis on the other. Lebanon has little to gain and much to lose by prolonging the conflict. A major windfall of the settlement would be to have the refugees settle elsewhere so they can no longer cause political instability in the country. Lebanon, no doubt, has tried to neutralize itself but was unable to do so. It is highly probable that the relation with the Palestinians will worsen rather than improve, and if so, the sooner the Lebanese reach a settlement the better. Lebanon can certainly play a major role by helping to reeducate the various parties regarding the possibilities of coexistence. They can also refrain from fanning the fire of war by ceasing to attack Israel or applaud the guerrillas for acts of terrorism and destruction. Lebanese intellectuals and statesmen can certainly make a great contribution simply by raising questions which so far have been intentionally left out of any debate. These questions, some of which I have raised above, must sooner or later reach the Arab press and be debated before realism can be reestablished. Lebanon is in a good position to promote such a debate.

Syria is more politically unstable than Lebanon and more warlike. Yet Syria can gain nothing from the war with Israel. The Syrians have already lost territory and caused many people to be dislocated. Regardless how long they delay a settlement, there is little gain that can be anticipated, other than recovering lost territory. It is possible that a change of attitude on the part of Syria would permit the recovery of the lost territory at a relatively low cost. Syria has the potential to help a settlement because of its size, contiguity, and the relatively small impact of the Palestinian Arabs in internal Syrian affairs. Syria can actually realize extensive benefits by pursuing a settlement. For example, there will be material saving on war expenditure; there will be a saving of lives of both Syrians and Palestinian Arabs; and there will be a chance for Syria to help the Palestinians settle on its land and thus benefit from their expertise in economic and agricultural development. By concentrating on a program of reconstruction, Syria might be able to stabilize its internal affairs and allow development to take place. If nothing else, Syria would be wise to reduce its warlike and aggressive attitude and concentrate on constructive ways of helping the Palestinians and themselves.

Iraq has usually complicated the Palestinian problem by rhetoric and by the inhumane treatment of Iraqi Jews. It probably could make a big contribution by simply acting generously in hosting Palestinians who might wish to settle there and by eliminating the political rhetoric they have excelled in for so long. The Iraqis have little to offer in the fight with Israel. At the same time they have land and resources which are crying for utilization and professional care.

The Palestinians can contribute if the Iraqis would act bravely and open their gates to them for settlement. In doing so, the Iraqis might be able to promote the idea of Arab nation and Arab unity more easily than by expending resources on a futile conflict with Israel. The history of Iraqi participation in that conflict suggests that a radical change in their approach might be useful, if only they will try.

As far as Saudi Arabia, Yemen, and the little Sheikhdoms are concerned, their main contribution would be to finance education and rehabilitation of the Palestinians and to open the doors for them to share in the economic advantages with which they are endowed. What the Palestinians will or should do can hardly be affected by these countries, which have neither the interest nor the power to fight Israel. Their sympathy with the Palestinians is mostly a function of the inter-Arab political dynamics rather than a reflection of their love for the Palestinians. Probably the same may be said of the North African Arab countries and Sudan. These countries are far away, and there is little hope or interest on their part to be active in the war with Israel, nor is there any real advantage to their being active. Their major contribution would be to let the Palestinians make their own decisions and give them the opportunity to share in the benefits these countries offer. There are vast areas in Sudan that may be settled; the Palestinians can do a lot there. Libyan oil offers opportunities of employment and development; Algerian oil may soon be in a similar position. Let the Palestinians share, instead of condoning a war that could at the most lead only to a larger share of the poverty Palestine can offer.

The fate of Jordan is so closely tied up with that of the Palestinians that they should be discussed jointly. Egypt, on the other hand, has miscalculated and lost three times already. In the process it has dragged others into defeat, especially in 1967. At the present time the main objective of

Egypt is to recover lost territory. There are indications that the cause of Palestine has faded into the background. It would be helpful if Egypt would be honest and brave enough to clarify its intentions. Rather than the apparent sell-out of the Palestinians, the Egyptians would be greatly helpful by openly fostering a policy of coexistence. In doing so, they would put an end to the misleading policy of the past. Egypt has reached a point that requires acting maturely and courageously, even though the political cost in the short run may be high. For example, Egypt could lead the Arab world in seeking alternatives to a repatriation which seems unworkable. Egypt could put an end to the inter-Arab massacre by removing the false hopes of the Palestinians, by leaving other Arab states to determine their own political affairs, and by concentrating on better use of the resources that the Arab world commands. By promoting cooperation, Egypt would help the Arab world to evolve toward unity; even the Palestinian conflict might be resolved in its favor.

Jordan has no political future separate from the Palestinians. A guerrilla war against Israel from Jordanian territory means coexistence between Jordan and Israel would be impossible. To prevent the guerrillas from acting violently would again lead to a civil war. Jordan is in a dilemma, and it seems inconceivable for King Hussein to withdraw from the conflict and reach a settlement with Israel independently from the Palestinians. Whatever arrangements are made, they would have to reconcile Jordanian and Palestinian interests. Some form of novelty in Jordanian politics might be necessary to allow the Palestinians a good share of responsibility in government; that would give them a vested interest in its stability. One such possibility might be to transform Jordan into a constitutional monarchy in which political parties run the government and bear the responsibilities. King Hussein would thus safeguard the monarchy and promote political stability in the country. An alternative approach might be for the King to give up the monarchy and to help to establish a republic. He could be the first president, or he could simply run for the presidency at the head of a political party. That would not only vindicate him before the Palestinians, but would make him a hero; it would also pull the rug from under those groups which are trying to undermine his monarchy. The people would then carry a larger share of the government of the country and bear the responsibility for its stability. The Palestinians would no longer be able to say that they have nothing more to lose; they will have their own republic.

Whichever solution is adopted, it would be preferable to the present state of affairs or to a separate Palestinian state, which would hardly be viable. King Hussein and the Palestinian leaders have much hard and deep thinking to do. A change of attitude is necessary. They have much to gain by making such a change. The Palestinian leaders need to show compassion to their own people. What can they promise those people and how would they deliver what they promise? It seems that they can sustain instability in the region: they are conducting a civil war in Jordan although they did not object to having Jordanian citizenship; they have brought havoc on southern Lebanon. The Palestinian leaders ought to know the limitations which they face in their fight with Israel and in their relations with the Arab countries. The models they have followed so far, the Algerian or the Viet Cong, do not apply in the fight against Israel. The Algerians were fighting a foreign power with a small minority of settlers. The Viet Cong are fighting an ideological war. Neither model can be fitted to the Arab-Israeli conflict. The Palestinian leaders need to be more creative in finding alternatives that may be viable. A coalition with King Hussein might be one; an autonomous state within a confederation might be another; the liquidation of the problem and adjustment as good citizens of the Arab countries in which they choose to live might be a third. To continue the present fruitless fight is not a viable alternative. The Palestinians are the ones who suffer, and their leaders bear the responsibility. Good leadership should reduce the suffering, not prolong it.

It is time that Israel stop acting like a spoiled child. Israel knows, and is constantly being reassured, that its benefactors will not abandon her. The United States will not impose a settlement, nor will it stop delivering arms. Israel continues to defy everybody by refusing to consider alternative approaches to settlement. It continues to set the conditions with little fear of losing friends or support. However, the spoiled child always pays for his follies. Israel must give up that attitude if it is to become politically and economically viable on its own and if it is to maintain a secure home for the Jewish people and a happy one for the youth of Israel.

It would be a great oversimplification to expect the Arabs and the Israelis to conclude a peace agreement and to become friends soon. They have too many bitter memories that will keep them apart for years to come. But I can imagine an Israel confined within legitimate borders, highly developed and prosperous, with no restrictions, fear, or insecurity. I can imagine Israelis speaking Arabic as well as Hebrew; I can see them visiting their Arab neighbors or playing hosts to them with respect and affection. That will be the nation I believed the forefathers of a Jewish national home to have in mind. That kind of Israel is far from reality, but it is possible. It is for the younger generation of Israelis to make that Israel a reality.

At the same time, I can see the younger Arabs freeing themselves of tradition and the rhetoric of blind and narrow nationalism. I can imagine an Arab nation in which the Palestinians can feel at home, whether they stay in Jordan or whether they explore and cultivate the rich soil of Iraq, the plains of Syria, or the riches of Kuwait and Libya. I can imagine young Palestinians rejecting the idle life of refugee camps; I can see them looking to a wider horizon in which opportunity abounds, rather than waste a lifetime fighting for a piece of real estate. The Palestinian Arabs have always been educationally and technically ahead of most others in the Arab world. Now it is time for them to show maturity and rationality in planning their future and the future of the coming generations. Man goes where his fortune awaits him, and so would they too, and be neither ashamed nor embarassed about adjusting to the dynamics of the Middle East and the people who populate it.

The Arabs and the Jews often boast of their cultural and moral superiority. The Arabs train their young to believe in kindness, generosity, wisdom, and alertness. They have the chance to show these great assets as Arab characteristics. The road to settlement is a way by which these assertions can be exemplified. At the same time, the Jews assert that they are chosen and unique as a people. They have the chance to show their uniqueness by serving the cause of peace. They can afford to be kind and even generous, not only to themselves but also to the other party. If both Arabs and Jews live up to their boasting, no doubt the future of these people can be bright, and they will be the ones to make it come true.[22]

[22]The literature on the conflict is immense. For those wishing to pursue the subject further, the following may be useful as background sources: David Waines, *The Unholy War: Israel and Palestine 1897–1971* (Wilmette, Ill.: Medina University Press International, 1971); Ralph H. Mangus, ed., *Documents on the Middle East* (Washington, D. C.: American Enterprise Institute, 1969); Richard H. Pfaff, *Jerusalem: Keystone of an Arab-Israeli Settlement* (Washington, D.C.: American Enterprise Institute, 1969); *Transactions*, vol. 7, no. 9–10 (July–August 1970), Special Issue, "The Permanent War Arabs vs. Israelis"; Henry Cattan, *Palestine, the Arabs, and Israel* (London: Longmans Green, 1969).

INDEX

Abdullah (king, son of King Hussein
  the First)
  and British, 21–23
Acre (town), 3, 67
Agriculture, 16, 69. *See also* Farming
Algeria, 5, 25, 49, 117
  and French, 51
All-Arab Palestinian Conference,
  17–18
American Friends Peace Conference,
  x
American Friends Society (Quakers),
  105
American Indians, 12, 14
Abdullah, Amir (king), negotiated
  with Golda Meir, 21–22
Anti-Semitism, 10, 30
  and the Western world, 10, 13
  attempts to gain sympathy, 10
Arabic language, 69, 110
Arabic literature, 51
Arab-Israelis. *See* Palenstinian Arabs
Arab-Israeli war
  as based on ignorance, 2
  beginnings of war in 1948, 9
  cost of war, 37–39, 87–88
  impact on daily life, 92
  losses in, 37–38
  pre-1948, 9–10
  as racial war, 10

  as religious war, 10–11, 12
  as territorial war, 11
Arab-Jewish-British conflict, 2–3
Arab League, 98–99
Arab press, 84
Arab rebels (Thuwārs), 3. *See also* Pal-
  stinian guerrillas
Arabs,
  as aggressors, 14
  and Arab refugees, 24–25, 58–59
  and Britain, 9, 21–23
  and British White Paper, 53
  brutality by, 3, 33–35
  claims of, 17–25 *passim*
  desire for land, 20
  economic differentiation, 19–20
  efforts for peace, 58–74 *passim*
  establishment of state of Israel,
    20–21
  foreign dominations of, 1, 9, 19
  as losers, 45
  losses of, 34
  and nationalism, 17, 18, 62, 63, 70
  national unity as myth, 17, 19–20
  points of recognition toward Arab-
    Israeli war, 84–90
  and Turkey, 9, 17, 21, 30
Armament industry, 31, 42, 108
  amount of aid from United States,
    57

121

Balfour Declaration, 20, 22, 28
  explained, 1
  promised a Jewish national home,
    13
Ben-Gurion, David, 45
Bi'na (village), 64
Blacks, of America, 12
Border problems, 15, 36, 45–48, 55,
    92
  ceded by Abdullah, 21
  de facto borders, 48, 52
  determined by United Nations,
    100–101
  June 5 boundaries, 73
  pre-1967, 15, 107
  as specified by Nasser, 71
  and United Nations, 51
Boundaries. See Border problems
Bourguiba (president of Tunisia), 25,
    55
  peace proposal, "gradualist ap-
    proach," 73–74
Boycott, by Arabs, 48, 86–87
Britain, 3, 26, 31
  and Arab rebellion, 9
  collaboration with Jews, 21–22
  Israel as puppet of, 49
  responsibilities of, 108–110
  and Turkish rebellion, 9
  and Uganda, 12
  withdrawl from Israel, 52–53
  and Zionist leaders, 22. See also
    Western powers
British Mandate, 17, 50–51, 53, 60

Canada, 30, 99
Capital, 15
  loss of human, 4, 37
  mobility of, 19–20
Capitalism, 10
Carmiel (town), 64–65
Ceasefires, 28, 95
  and United Nations, 78
Childers, Erskine B. ("Impasse in the
    Holy Land"), 78–79
Children, supporting parents, 66
China, 33, 93
  aid to war, 41
  and United States policy, 84

Christians, 19, 46, 56
  and Palestine, 12
Churchill, Winston, 49
Citrus production, by Arabs, 16
Classical imperialism, 6. See also Im-
    perialism
Cold war, 27, 31–33
  effects on peace, 83
Colonialism, 49
Compromises, need for, 4
Construction, by Israeli Arabs, 63
Cultural annihilation, 69
Cyprus, 49
Czechoslovakia, 28

de Gaulle, and Algerian War, 5
Deir al Asad (village), 64
Dislocation of people. See Refugees
Druzism, 19

East Jerusalem, 79, 80
Eban, Aba
  address to United Nations General
    Assembly, 55–56
  on peacemaking, 54–55, 72, 73
  on refugees, 56
  on United Nations Partition Plan,
    76
Education, 62, 84
  of Israeli Arabs, 50, 64, 119
Egypt, 19, 22, 23, 37–38, 67
  and cold war, 111
  cost of war to, 40
  and Jewish immigration, 73
  as most powerful Arab country, 20
  peace proposals by, 70–72
  role in war, 115–116
  and waterways, 101–102
Elath (seaport), 79
Eshkol (prime minister), on peace-
    making, 55
Expansionism, 15. See also Jews, as ex-
    pansionists

Farming, 14
  by Israeli Arabs, 64–66. See also
    Agriculture
Fascism, 8
Feisal (king of Iraq), 22

Royal Commission, 21
Russell, Bertrand, on war, 8

Safad, 22
SAMs II and III, 32, 109. *See also* Armament industry
Sharm-el-Sheikh, 80, 92
Saudi Arabia, 19
  role in war, 115
Sharett, Moshe (foreign minister), on peacemaking, 54
Sinai, 36, 92
Skeikhdoms, 115
Socialism, 10
Soviet Russia, 15, 31, 81, 93
  as anti-semitic, 29–30
  and destruction of State of Israel, 85
  military aid to Egypt, 40, 41
  and 1956 Suez crisis, 5
  responsibility of, 108–110
Spain, 12
State of Israel, 18, 80, 85–86
  concept of national home, 1, 6, 7, 90
  creation of, 9, 13–14
  features of, 15
  and Palestinian Arabs, 50
  as a sovereign nation, 96
  tenth anniversary of the, 51
Straits of Tiran, 102
Sudan, 49, 115
Suez Canal, 15, 36, 79–80, 102
  and the ceasefire, 57, 72
  invasion of, by Jews, 15
Syria, 18, 19, 22, 37–38, 41, 86, 119
  cost of war to, 40
  and Golan Heights, 80
  nationalism, 24
  and refugee problem, 46

Tiberius, 22
Tobacco products, by Arabs, 16, 65
Turkey, 12, 21, 30
  and Cyprus, 51
  as power in Middle East, 26–27
  and recognition of Israel, 111

Unemployment, 67
  affected by war, 88

United Nations, 27, 31, 71
  appeals to, from American Friends Society, 105
  and arms-producing powers, 109
  and borders, 15, 51, 52, 100
  and China, 84
  concern for peace, 57
  history of peacemaking efforts, 76–78
  and legitimacy of Israeli state, 53
  partition plan of, 1947, 47, 48, 60, 68, 75, 76
  and refugees, 98
  resolution 194, of, 46, 47
  responsibility of, 106–108
  structure of, 74
  weakness of, 74–75
United Nations Security Council, 73, 74
United States, 15, 26, 28, 31, 39, 111, 118
  aid level compared, 38
  antagonism with Israel, 92
  armament aid from, 57, 104
  and China, 84
  committment to Israel, 86
  concern for peace, 57
  Israel as puppet of, 49
  and refugees, 99
  responsibility of, 108–110
United Syrian government, 18

Viet Cong, 117
Vietnam, 38

War,
  as moral, 8–9
  as immoral, 7–8, 26
Waterways, 56, 71, 101–102
  navigation guarantee of, by U.N., 77
Weizmann, Haim, supporter of Balfour Declaration, 22
Welfare program, 100
West Bank, 79
Western powers, 14, 16
  as anti-semitic, 13, 26
  and the defeat of Turkey, 27
  and encouragement of war, 41–42